ELECTRONICS

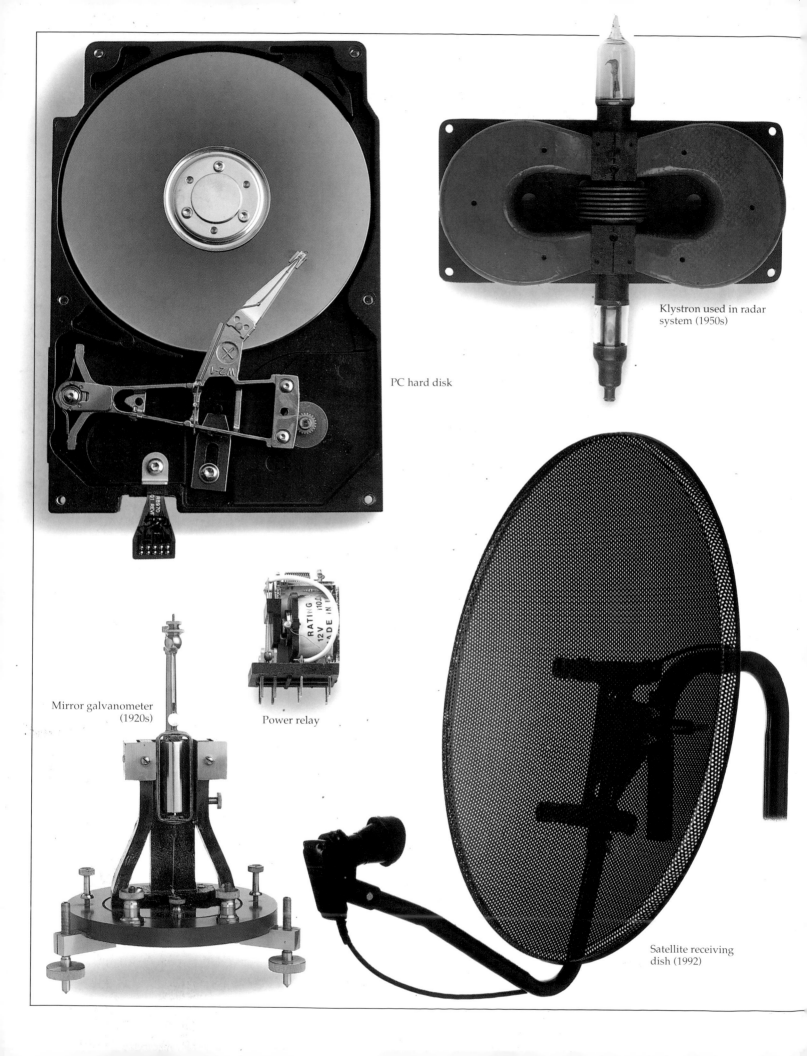

PC hard disk

Klystron used in radar system (1950s)

Mirror galvanometer (1920s)

Power relay

Satellite receiving dish (1992)

Interference
suppressor
capacitor

Signal transistor

EYEWITNESS 👁 GUIDES

ELECTRONICS

Written by
ROGER BRIDGMAN

PC memory board

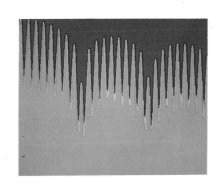
Spectrum of a pulse signal

Audio output transformer

Small
packaged
integrated
circuit

Silicon chips

B.B.C.
TELEVISION O.Bs.
(LONDON)

BBC-Marconi
AXBT ribbon
microphone
(1950s)

Pocket computer
(1990s)

DK

DORLING KINDERSLEY
LONDON • NEW YORK • SYDNEY
in association with
THE SCIENCE MUSEUM, LONDON

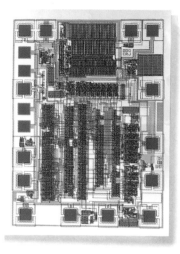

Print-out of a pattern
for an integrated circuit

First microphone, made
by David Hughes in 1878

Thyristor for
power control

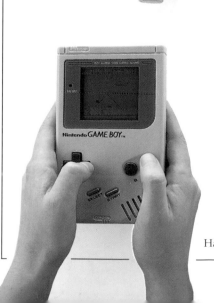

Hand-held video game

Dorling Kindersley

**LONDON, NEW YORK, AUCKLAND, DELHI, JOHANNESBURG,
MUNICH, PARIS and SYDNEY**

For a full catalogue, visit

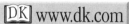 **www.dk.com**

Project editor Charyn Jones
Art editor Ron Stobbart
Design assistant Helen Diplock
Production Louise Daly
Picture research Deborah Pownall
Managing editor Josephine Buchanan
Managing art editor Lynne Brown
Special photography Clive Streeter
Editorial consultant Eryl Davies,
the Science Museum, London

This Eyewitness ®/™ Guide
first published in Great Britain in 1993 by
Dorling Kindersley Limited, 9 Henrietta Street,
London WC2E 8PS

2 4 6 8 10 9 7 5 3 1

Copyright © 1993
Dorling Kindersley Limited, London

A CIP catalogue record for this book is available
from the British Library

ISBN 0-7513-6145-3

Colour reproduction by Colourscan, Singapore
Printed in China by Toppan Printing Co. (Shenzhen) Ltd.

Headphones (1920s)

Miniature valve
(1960s)

Loudspeaker for use
with a radio (1920s)

Contents

Large electromagnet used with the first magnetron for radar (p. 40)

What is electronics?

ELECTRONIC DEVICES CAN MAKE SOUNDS, send messages, show pictures, measure, remember, calculate, and control. Machines made from wheels and levers can do some of these things, but they are often too slow and clumsy to do them well. Electricity can be used to power such machines, but this does not make them electronic. A machine can claim this title only if it contains devices in which the motion of the tiny particles called electrons that form electric currents can be directly influenced by electricity or magnetism. Devices of this kind allow electricity to control electricity itself. In a television set, for example, electricity from the aerial controls currents that paint pictures on the screen (pp. 44-45). In a computer, electrical changes caused by pressing keys control the power that writes data to a disk. Using electricity in this way makes it possible to do complicated things quickly and inexpensively. Ordinary machines are good for simple, repetitive jobs like drilling holes or drying hair. But if you want a versatile machine that can instantly change its behaviour in response to incoming information, you need electronics. A device like a radio can make a limitless range of sounds and a powerful electronic computer can conjure up an infinity of imaginary worlds.

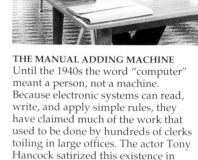

THE MANUAL ADDING MACHINE
Until the 1940s the word "computer" meant a person, not a machine. Because electronic systems can read, write, and apply simple rules, they have claimed much of the work that used to be done by hundreds of clerks toiling in large offices. The actor Tony Hancock satirized this existence in the 1961 film *The Rebel*.

Terminal

Resistor

Switch hook opens line circuit when handset is replaced

Handset cord

Hand wiring

Electromagnet

Rotary dial

Handset

Bell

ELECTROMECHANICAL TELEPHONE
The telephone has been a vital part of communications for over a century, and both electrical and electronic techniques have played a part in its development. The traditional instrument is electric, not electronic. It includes nothing that can control electricity electrically. To dial, a disc is rotated, winding up a spring that operates moving contacts to signal numbers to the exchange. Incoming calls are signalled by a hammer, moved by electromagnets, hitting a pair of bells. There is no memory. Speech is amplified (pp. 30-31) by the microphone inside the handset (pp. 42-43). Telephones of this type are the direct descendants of instruments designed in the 19th century, long before electronics was thought of, but they are still in service all over the world.

Quartz crystal for frequency control

Filter removes unwanted signals

Integrated circuit processes radio signals

Loudspeaker | Keyboard | Percussion pad

RADIO PAGER
Except for large organizations like the police, keeping in touch electronically started with the radio pager, which merely listens out for its own call sign and bleeps when it detects it. In the 1970s even a simple gadget like this was rare. Now, with sophisticated technology readily available, the pager is seen as the poor person's mobile phone.

MAKING MUSICAL SOUNDS
Every musical instrument has a characteristic sound which depends on the frequencies (pp. 14-15) it produces and the way its notes start and stop. Once a sound has been analyzed, electronic devices can mimic it using oscillators, amplifiers, and filters (pp. 34-35). Notes from actual instruments can be recorded in electronic memory to be retrieved and manipulated using the keyboard. Electronics can even produce sounds that never existed before.

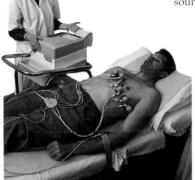

HEART MONITOR
Muscles like the heart produce electrical effects when they work. Electronics can make this activity visible to doctors. The electrocardiograph amplifies and records electrical signals from the heart, picked up by contacts on the patient's body – just one of the many medical applications of electronics.

Switch hook opens line circuit when handset is replaced

ELECTRON MICROGRAPH
Electronics is about controlling fundamental electrical particles called electrons (pp. 26-27). One thing they can do is form magnified images. Electrons can show far smaller details than the light used by ordinary microscopes. This colour-enhanced picture was made by scanning the subject with a beam of electrons.

A flea magnified 30 times

Printed circuit board

Printed circuit board

Keypad

ELECTRONIC TELEPHONE
Modern telephones are full of electrical control devices called transistors (pp. 38-39), so are truly electronic. They use oscillators (pp. 32-33) to signal numbers by generating tones when the keys are pressed. An oscillator and transducer (pp. 42-43) replace the heavy bells of older telephones, giving the distinctive warbling sound of the electronic telephone. The last number dialled is held in an electronic memory (pp. 56-57) and an electronic amplifier boosts the small signal coming from a lightweight microphone. The components are built into the printed circuit boards.

Handset

The pre-electric world

Around 1840 electricity started to change the way people lived. Messages from the electric telegraph (pp. 24-25) began to replace letters brought by horse or ship, and electric power followed soon after. But machines to help people communicate with each other, control things, and do calculations have existed for a long time. In these simple machines lie the beginnings of some basic ideas used in electronics – principles like logic, amplification, and memory. The machines worked slowly and cost a lot to build and run. Many broke down – their ropes, levers, or wheels wore out in time. Communication devices were primitive. At night, you could signal "yes" or "no" by lighting or not lighting a fire. This idea of a code based on just two possibilities lives on today at the heart of every digital electronic system.

GUIDING SPEECH
Normal speech has limited range because it spreads out in all directions, wasting most of its power. But sound can be channelled through tubes over short distances, so large houses used to have speaking tubes to direct the power to where it was needed, usually from the family's quarters to the servants' quarters.

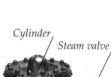

Millions row

Black bead helps counting

Quarters row

Frame

Rope controlling pull

ANCIENT CALCULATOR
The abacus is an elegant calculating aid that probably originated in ancient Babylon. The beads of this Russian abacus, or *stchoty*, are designed to count money. The top row counts millions, the next hundreds of thousands, and so on. Expert users can often beat an electronic calculator to the correct answer.

STEERING A TRUE COURSE
The person at the helm of this ocean-going yacht watches the compass and uses the rudder to correct any deviation from the desired course. The helm acts as an amplifier, feeding back information from the compass to control the mighty power of wind and sea.

Cylinder

Steam valve

Connecting rod

Brake handle

Drum

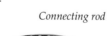

AMPLIFYING A SIGNAL
Capstans are used to move heavy weights by means of ropes or chains. They are turned continuously by powerful engines, but will not pull on a load until the rope is tightened around the drum by a much gentler pull from its operator. In the same way, although an audio amplifier is plugged into the electricity socket all the time, power only reaches the speakers under the control of a tiny signal from something like a compact disc player.

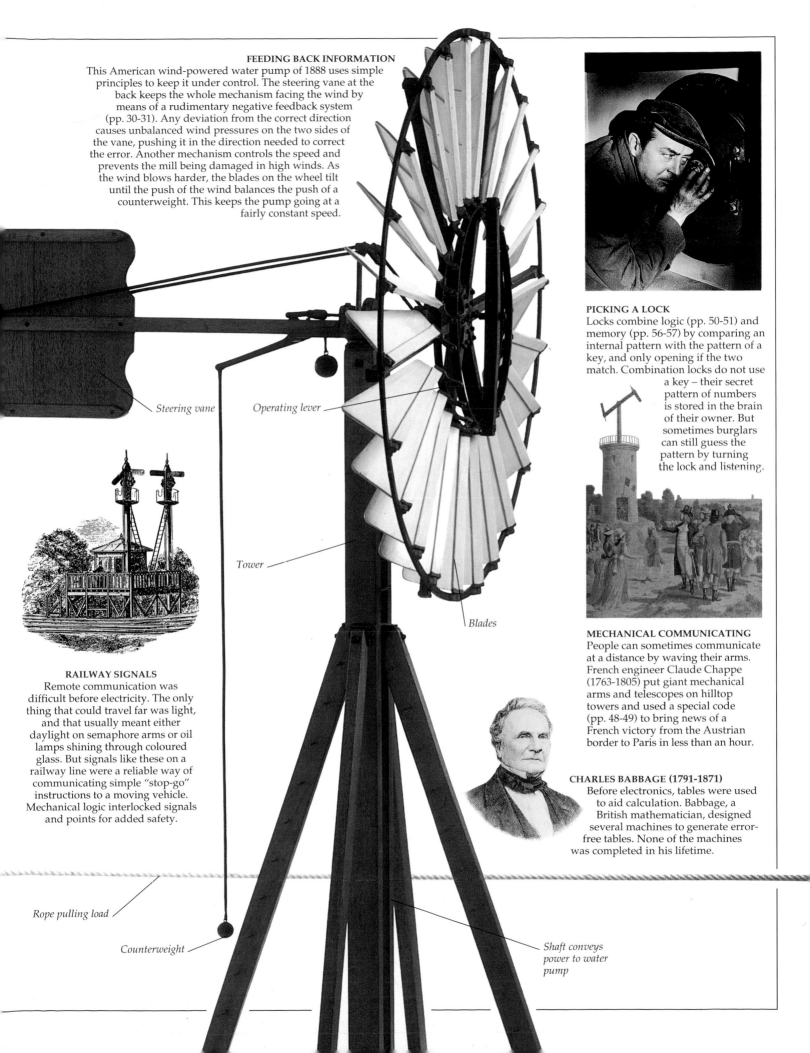

FEEDING BACK INFORMATION

This American wind-powered water pump of 1888 uses simple principles to keep it under control. The steering vane at the back keeps the whole mechanism facing the wind by means of a rudimentary negative feedback system (pp. 30-31). Any deviation from the correct direction causes unbalanced wind pressures on the two sides of the vane, pushing it in the direction needed to correct the error. Another mechanism controls the speed and prevents the mill being damaged in high winds. As the wind blows harder, the blades on the wheel tilt until the push of the wind balances the push of a counterweight. This keeps the pump going at a fairly constant speed.

Steering vane

Operating lever

Tower

Blades

PICKING A LOCK

Locks combine logic (pp. 50-51) and memory (pp. 56-57) by comparing an internal pattern with the pattern of a key, and only opening if the two match. Combination locks do not use a key – their secret pattern of numbers is stored in the brain of their owner. But sometimes burglars can still guess the pattern by turning the lock and listening.

MECHANICAL COMMUNICATING

People can sometimes communicate at a distance by waving their arms. French engineer Claude Chappe (1763-1805) put giant mechanical arms and telescopes on hilltop towers and used a special code (pp. 48-49) to bring news of a French victory from the Austrian border to Paris in less than an hour.

CHARLES BABBAGE (1791-1871)

Before electronics, tables were used to aid calculation. Babbage, a British mathematician, designed several machines to generate error-free tables. None of the machines was completed in his lifetime.

RAILWAY SIGNALS

Remote communication was difficult before electricity. The only thing that could travel far was light, and that usually meant either daylight on semaphore arms or oil lamps shining through coloured glass. But signals like these on a railway line were a reliable way of communicating simple "stop-go" instructions to a moving vehicle. Mechanical logic interlocked signals and points for added safety.

Rope pulling load

Counterweight

Shaft conveys power to water pump

Electricity and magnetism

ELECTRICITY AND MAGNETISM are closely intertwined. Two of the greatest discoveries of the 19th century were that a wire carrying an electric current acts like a magnet and that a change of magnetism can make current flow. (Putting the two together, this also means that a changing current in one wire can make current flow in another.) These discoveries have had an enormous effect on everyday life. They have allowed us to build generators that can convert the energy in fuels like coal or oil into abundant electric power, using wires with currents flowing in them as magnets and whirling them past other wires to create even bigger currents. Just a little of this power goes into electronic devices. By exploiting the intimate relationship between magnetism and electricity, electronic devices can make music, pictures, or even radio waves.

PIONEER OF ELECTRICITY
Michael Faraday (1791-1867) rose from a poor family to become one of the greatest scientists of his day. Working in London at the Royal Institution, he made many fundamental discoveries in chemistry and physics. In 1831, having read about the work of Oersted (p. 11), he discovered that changing magnetism near a wire causes current to flow, completing the link between magnetism and electricity.

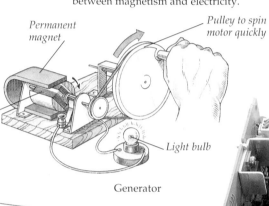

Permanent magnet

Wire wound on armature

Pulley to spin motor quickly

Light bulb

Generator

MEASURING CURRENT
Tangent galvanometers used Oersted's discovery to measure current. The instrument was turned until the coil pointed the same way as the compass needle. Current passed through the coil then created magnetism at right angles to the magnetism of the Earth, and the needle swung to a new angle that showed the strength of the current. This galvanometer was made in Britain in about 1900.

Small magnet for fine adjustment

Battery

Electric motor

Commutator reverses current in wires as armature rotates

THE MOTOR AND GENERATOR
An electric motor normally converts electrical energy into mechanical work. With a battery connected to the motor, currents in the wires create magnetism that pushes against the permanent magnet, making the armature spin and turning the handle. If the battery is replaced by a bulb, and the handle turned to spin the armature, the motor becomes a generator. Currents induced as the wires move past the magnet make the bulb light up. As Faraday realized, electricity and magnetism can sometimes change places.

Permanent magnet

Wire wound on armature

Short compass needle

Coil

Connecting terminal

Scale graduated in degrees

USING ELECTRICITY AND MAGNETISM
Like a television set, a video recorder (VCR) receives signals from a television station or cable. But instead of turning them into pictures, the VCR stores them on magnetic tape. The process is much the same as recording sound (pp. 52-53). The VCR relies heavily on magnetism and electricity. It uses the magnetic push of current-carrying wires in an electric motor to spin a drum at high speed and move the tape slowly past it. To record a programme, currents flowing through coils of wire inside the drum are used to create magnetic patterns on the tape. When the tape is played back, the recorder uses these magnetic patterns to produce currents which a television set can turn into pictures.

Video recorder (late 1970s)

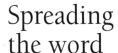

Without Oersted's famous observation of 1820 electricity and magnetism might have remained separate and mysterious subjects. Oersted published his findings in 1821, enabling Michael Faraday (p. 10) and later James Maxwell (p. 12) to do the work that led to the generation of electric power and the discovery of radio waves. Joseph Henry (pp. 18-19) used Oersted's work to understand how magnetic components such as inductors behave. Building on this, Oliver Heaviside (p. 13) explained how electric signals travel through long cables, extending the speed and range of international communication.

Terminal connecting to battery

Loop of wire

Wooden base

Angle of needle can increase to 90° with strong enough current

Terminal

Magnetic compass needle

HANS CHRISTIAN OERSTED (1777-1851)
Oersted was a Danish scientist who made the discovery that linked magnetism to electricity and pointed physics toward a deeper understanding of these subjects. But scientists of his day did not always stick to one science. Oersted was the first person to prepare aluminium as a pure metal, and he also isolated piperine, the chemical that makes pepper peppery.

OERSTED'S COMPASS
Lecturing at the University of Copenhagen in 1820, Oersted connected a battery to a wire which happened to run near the needle of a compass. The magnetic needle swung around, and Oersted immediately realized the significance of this. The current-carrying wire was acting as a magnet, revealing that magnetism and electricity were related.

Erase head prepares tape for new recording

Angled, spinning drum carrying two record/playback heads

Tape records pictures as magnetic stripes

Sound record/playback head

Capstan rotates to feed tape past drum

Motor driven by pulses that keep drum in step with pictures

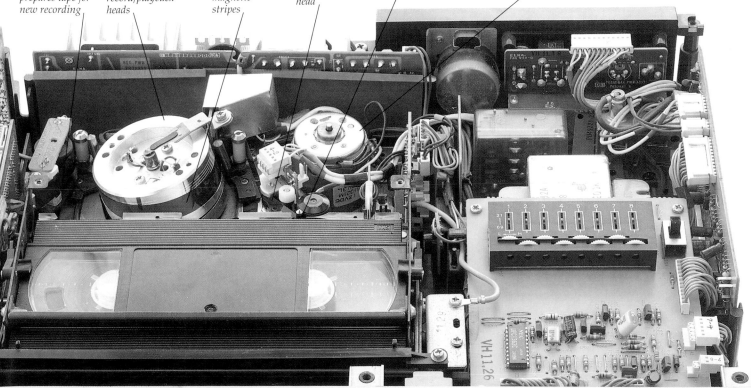

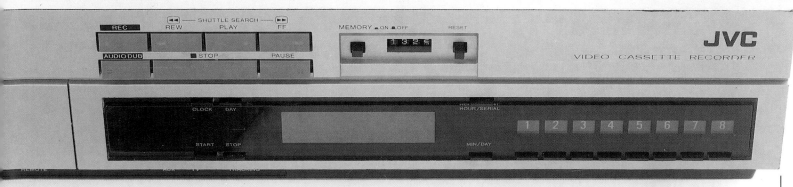

Electromagnetic waves

WAVES ARE ALL AROUND US, rippling on water, rolling across a field of corn or keeping a centipede's legs organized – as well as bringing us sound and light. Waves allow something to go from one place to another without anything moving very much, making them of vital importance to communication. Waves usually occur in a medium that can store and pass on energy in two different but related forms. Sound, for instance, can travel in anything able to store energy as motion and pressure. For electromagnetic waves the medium is space itself, which can store energy in electric and magnetic form. Scottish mathematician James Clerk Maxwell (1831-1879) extended the work done by Michael Faraday (p. 10). He realized that the close relationship between electricity and magnetism made this kind of wave possible. His calculations showed that the wave would travel at the speed of light, making him suspect that light itself was an electromagnetic wave. In 1888 Heinrich Hertz generated waves electrically and showed that they behave just like light, confirming Faraday's and Maxwell's ideas.

PROVING WAVES EXIST
In 1886, at Karlsruhe in Germany, physicist Heinrich Hertz (1857-1894) set out to see if Maxwell was right about the existence of radio waves. He made high-voltage sparks jump between two rods and noticed that tiny sparks jumped across a gap between two other rods some distance away, suggesting that electromagnetic waves were crossing the room. Using flat and curved reflectors, wooden prisms, and many other devices, Hertz was able to show that the waves behave very much like light.

WAVE MACHINE
There are two ways of looking at a wave: either focusing on a fixed point, or following the shape of the wave as it travels. Every point goes through the same cycle of changes, but a point a little farther from the source of the wave goes through its cycle a little later. The wave shape is the combined effect of all the points doing the same thing slightly out of step. This model demonstrates wave motion using pivoted slats linked by springs. As each slat swings, it stretches a spring, moving the next slat. The speed of the wave depends on the properties of the slats and springs, just as the speed of electromagnetic waves is governed by the electric and magnetic properties of space.

WAVES MAKING THINGS HAPPEN
When a metal disc strikes a closely packed and firmly held line of discs, a loose one at the far end shoots off. A pressure wave in the metal, travelling much faster than the moving disc, carries its energy down the line. In a similar way, when a bulb is connected to a battery, an electromagnetic wave tells the bulb to start glowing long before any electrons from the battery get there.

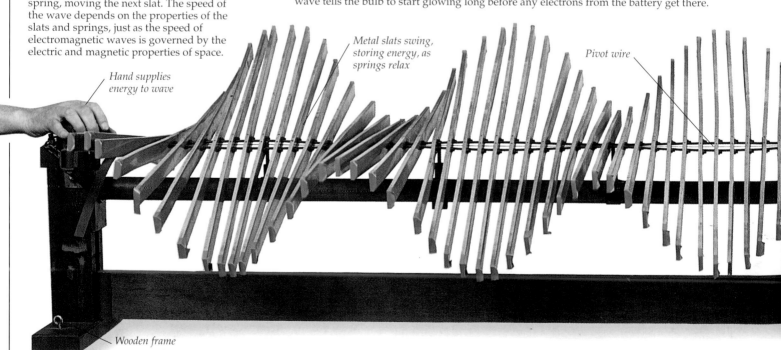

Hand supplies energy to wave

Metal slats swing, storing energy, as springs relax

Pivot wire

Wooden frame

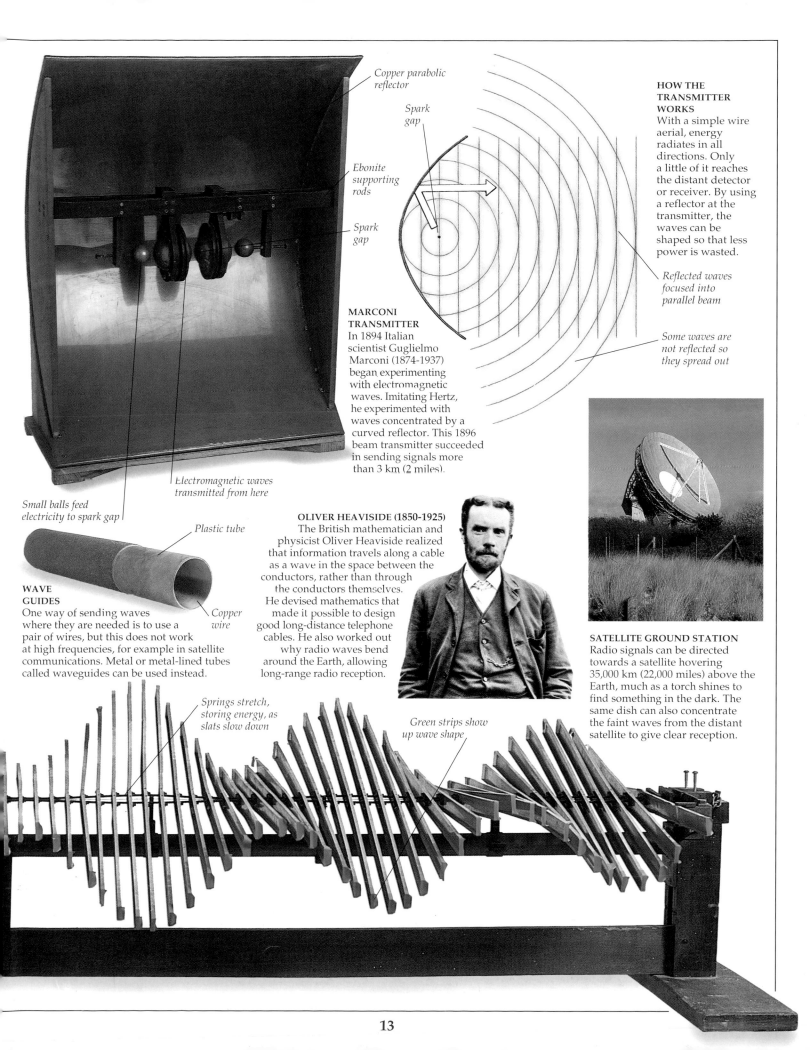

Copper parabolic
reflector

Spark
gap

Ebonite
supporting
rods

Spark
gap

**HOW THE
TRANSMITTER
WORKS**
With a simple wire
aerial, energy
radiates in all
directions. Only
a little of it reaches
the distant detector
or receiver. By using
a reflector at the
transmitter, the
waves can be
shaped so that less
power is wasted.

*Reflected waves
focused into
parallel beam*

*Some waves are
not reflected so
they spread out*

**MARCONI
TRANSMITTER**
In 1894 Italian
scientist Guglielmo
Marconi (1874-1937)
began experimenting
with electromagnetic
waves. Imitating Hertz,
he experimented with
waves concentrated by a
curved reflector. This 1896
beam transmitter succeeded
in sending signals more
than 3 km (2 miles).

*Electromagnetic waves
transmitted from here*

*Small balls feed
electricity to spark gap*

Plastic tube

**WAVE
GUIDES**
One way of sending waves
where they are needed is to use a
pair of wires, but this does not work
at high frequencies, for example in satellite
communications. Metal or metal-lined tubes
called waveguides can be used instead.

*Copper
wire*

OLIVER HEAVISIDE (1850-1925)
The British mathematician and
physicist Oliver Heaviside realized
that information travels along a cable
as a wave in the space between the
conductors, rather than through
the conductors themselves.
He devised mathematics that
made it possible to design
good long-distance telephone
cables. He also worked out
why radio waves bend
around the Earth, allowing
long-range radio reception.

SATELLITE GROUND STATION
Radio signals can be directed
towards a satellite hovering
35,000 km (22,000 miles) above the
Earth, much as a torch shines to
find something in the dark. The
same dish can also concentrate
the faint waves from the distant
satellite to give clear reception.

*Springs stretch,
storing energy, as
slats slow down*

*Green strips show
up wave shape*

The importance of frequency

ELECTROMAGNETIC WAVES go through a continual cycle of changing electricity and magnetism. Any pattern or wave that repeats in this way has a frequency – the number of repeats per second – and every radio dial shows how important frequency is in electronics. Equally important are the changing shapes of waves, which enable them to carry information. Electronics engineers deal with the infinite variety of possible shapes by describing them in terms of a limited range of frequencies. A wave of any shape can be thought of as a combination of simpler waves of a standard shape. The recipe listing the frequencies, strengths, and relative timing of the waves making up a particular shape is called its spectrum. Breaking complex waves down into their basic ingredients like this makes it much easier to understand and design electronic systems.

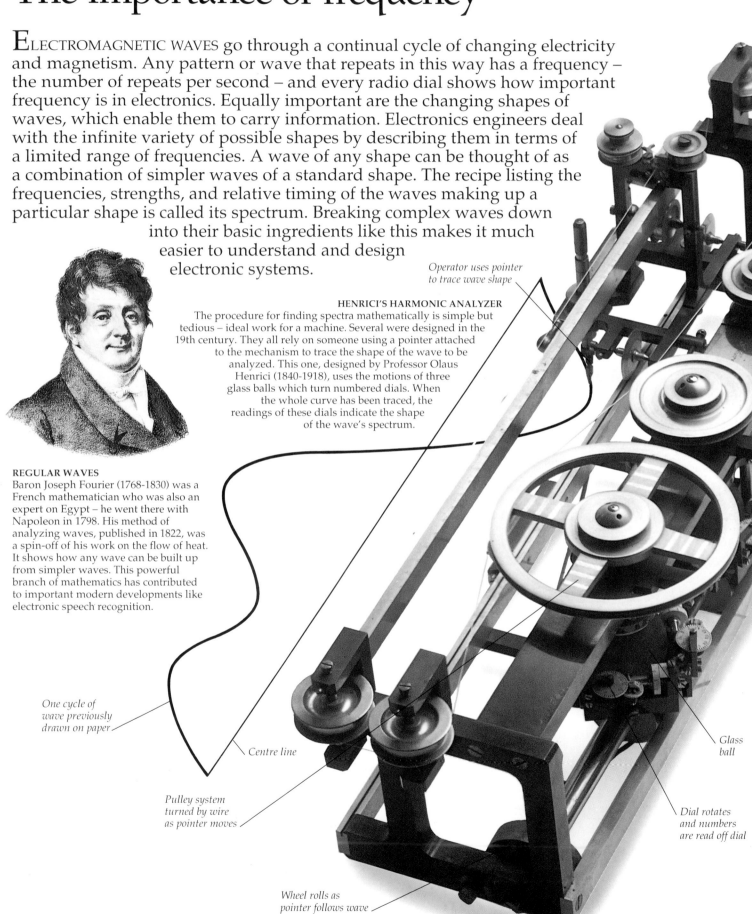

HENRICI'S HARMONIC ANALYZER
The procedure for finding spectra mathematically is simple but tedious – ideal work for a machine. Several were designed in the 19th century. They all rely on someone using a pointer attached to the mechanism to trace the shape of the wave to be analyzed. This one, designed by Professor Olaus Henrici (1840-1918), uses the motions of three glass balls which turn numbered dials. When the whole curve has been traced, the readings of these dials indicate the shape of the wave's spectrum.

Operator uses pointer to trace wave shape

REGULAR WAVES
Baron Joseph Fourier (1768-1830) was a French mathematician who was also an expert on Egypt – he went there with Napoleon in 1798. His method of analyzing waves, published in 1822, was a spin-off of his work on the flow of heat. It shows how any wave can be built up from simpler waves. This powerful branch of mathematics has contributed to important modern developments like electronic speech recognition.

One cycle of wave previously drawn on paper

Centre line

Pulley system turned by wire as pointer moves

Glass ball

Dial rotates and numbers are read off dial

Wheel rolls as pointer follows wave

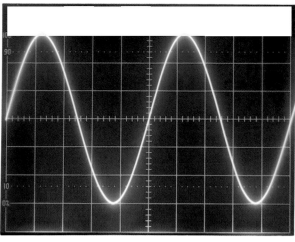

SINE WAVE
This smooth, simple curve is called a sine wave. It is the basic shape into which more complex waves are analyzed by Fourier's method. It is displayed by an oscilloscope, an instrument that produces a graph showing how voltage varies with time. Harmonic oscillators (pp. 32-33) of all kinds generate an output like this.

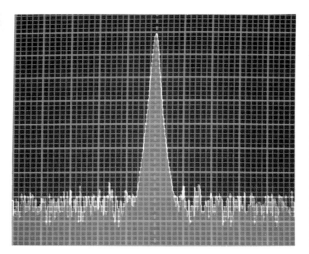

SINE WAVE SPECTRUM
Most waves can be thought of as made from several sine waves of different frequencies. A spectrum analyzer, used to display this picture, is an instrument that produces a graph showing how much of each frequency is present. A pure sine wave contains only one frequency, which shows up on the analyzer as a single peak.

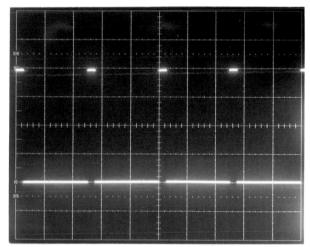

PULSES
Pulses are on/off signals, reproduced here from an oscilloscope screen. Simple, repeated pulses like these can be used for timing in clocks, television, or computers. More complicated sequences of pulses can form a code (pp. 46-49) to represent information in computers and communication systems.

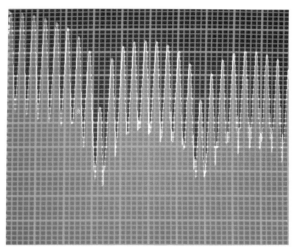

PULSE SPECTRUM
Although these pulses repeat at a similar frequency to the sine wave (above left), their sharp, narrow shape means that they also contain a large number of higher frequency components. These show up on the spectrum analyzer screen as a characteristic pattern of peaks.

SWINGING OF A PENDULUM
The Italian astronomer Galileo Galilei (1564-1642) observed that pendulums swing at a constant frequency and so can be used to make clocks. Knowing the number of ticks per second, it is only necessary to count the ticks to keep track of time. Galileo designed his pendulum clock in 1642, but this one was built in 1883 from drawings made later. Quartz clocks use the same idea, although the quartz crystal vibrates at a much higher frequency than a pendulum.

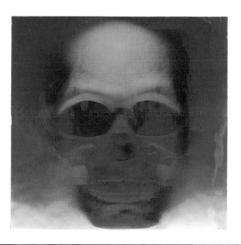

LIGHT SPECTRUM
Our eyes respond only to the frequency and intensity of light waves, not their shape. When white light is split into its components, as in this hologram, the highest frequencies register as violet and the lowest as red. The simple way the eye analyzes light allows any colour to be matched using just three frequencies, making colour television (pp. 44-45) a practical possibility.

Resistors

IN ELECTRONICS, RESISTANCE PROVIDED BY RESISTORS plays the part of friction. Friction is sometimes a nuisance, but life would be difficult without it – wheels and feet would not grip the road, brakes would not stop cars, things would slide out of control. Without resistance, there would be a similar lack of control in electronic circuits. Electric currents are caused by the voltages that arise when there are different amounts of electricity in different parts of a circuit. When such a voltage starts to drive current through a resistor, another voltage appears between its ends, pushing against the driving voltage and limiting the current. This effect is sometimes used directly, for example to prevent light-emitting diodes (pp. 44-45) burning out. More often, the voltages set up by currents in resistors are used to convey information, or to help other components such as transistors (pp. 38-39) do their job. Like brakes and clutches, their frictional equivalents in machines, resistors get hot when they work because they exert control by wasting power as heat. They can only reduce the power of an electrical signal, never increase it.

OHM'S LAW
German physicist Georg Simon Ohm (1787-1854) found that the current in a conductor is always equal to the voltage between its ends divided by a fixed number, its resistance. The unit of resistance – the ohm, indicated by the symbol Ω – is named after him.

Cable controls pressure of brake block on wheel

Terminal

Bypass plug

BRAKING
The speed of a bicycle coasting down hill is limited by friction, which produces a force opposing gravity and increasing with speed. When friction balances gravity the bike stops accelerating. Resistors can control current from a battery by producing opposing voltages that increase with current. When the power is switched on, current increases until the resistor voltages balance the battery voltage.

Brake block rubs against wheel to control friction

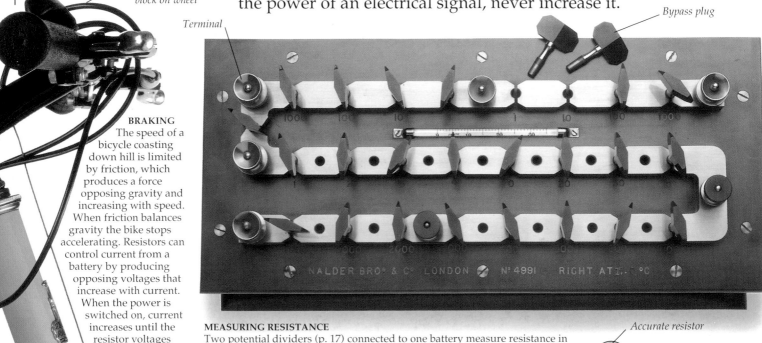

NALDER BROS & Cᵒ LONDON   Nᵒ 4991   RIGHT AT 1.0 °C

MEASURING RESISTANCE
Two potential dividers (p. 17) connected to one battery measure resistance in this 19th-century circuit, known as a Wheatstone bridge. The resistor to be measured and a resistor with a known value make one divider. Two more known resistors form the other. When the divider voltages are equal, so that a meter bridging between them reads zero, the resistor ratios in both dividers must be the same, giving the value of the unknown resistor. Modern instruments use the same principle. To use this bridge, the unknown resistor, battery, and meter are connected to terminals, and resistors inside the box are brought into play by pulling out plugs that normally bypass them.

Accurate resistor

Unknown resistor

Accurate resistor

Arrow shows direction and strength of current

Battery

Meter

Accurate resistor

Redness indicates voltage

Principle of Wheatstone bridge

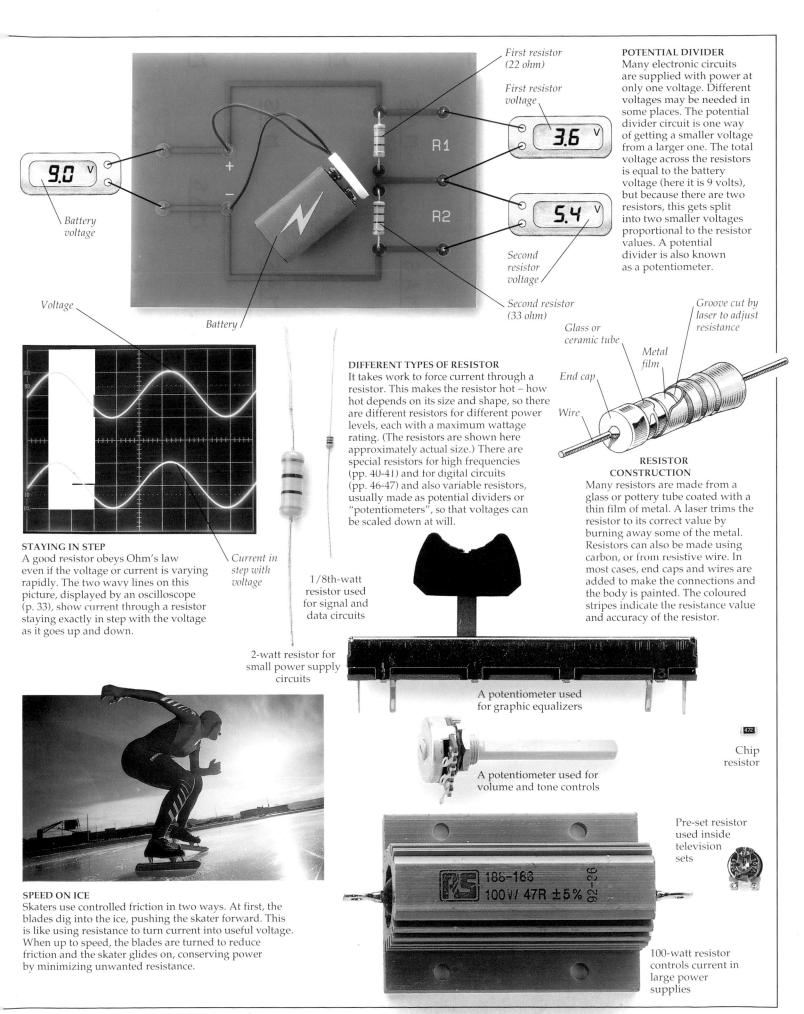

First resistor (22 ohm)

First resistor voltage

3.6 V

R1

9.0 V

Battery voltage

+ −

R2

5.4 V

Second resistor voltage

Second resistor (33 ohm)

Battery

POTENTIAL DIVIDER
Many electronic circuits are supplied with power at only one voltage. Different voltages may be needed in some places. The potential divider circuit is one way of getting a smaller voltage from a larger one. The total voltage across the resistors is equal to the battery voltage (here it is 9 volts), but because there are two resistors, this gets split into two smaller voltages proportional to the resistor values. A potential divider is also known as a potentiometer.

Groove cut by laser to adjust resistance

Glass or ceramic tube

Metal film

End cap

Wire

RESISTOR CONSTRUCTION
Many resistors are made from a glass or pottery tube coated with a thin film of metal. A laser trims the resistor to its correct value by burning away some of the metal. Resistors can also be made using carbon, or from resistive wire. In most cases, end caps and wires are added to make the connections and the body is painted. The coloured stripes indicate the resistance value and accuracy of the resistor.

Voltage

DIFFERENT TYPES OF RESISTOR
It takes work to force current through a resistor. This makes the resistor hot – how hot depends on its size and shape, so there are different resistors for different power levels, each with a maximum wattage rating. (The resistors are shown here approximately actual size.) There are special resistors for high frequencies (pp. 40-41) and for digital circuits (pp. 46-47) and also variable resistors, usually made as potential dividers or "potentiometers", so that voltages can be scaled down at will.

Current in step with voltage

STAYING IN STEP
A good resistor obeys Ohm's law even if the voltage or current is varying rapidly. The two wavy lines on this picture, displayed by an oscilloscope (p. 33), show current through a resistor staying exactly in step with the voltage as it goes up and down.

1/8th-watt resistor used for signal and data circuits

2-watt resistor for small power supply circuits

A potentiometer used for graphic equalizers

A potentiometer used for volume and tone controls

Chip resistor

Pre-set resistor used inside television sets

186-166
100W 47R ±5%

100-watt resistor controls current in large power supplies

SPEED ON ICE
Skaters use controlled friction in two ways. At first, the blades dig into the ice, pushing the skater forward. This is like using resistance to turn current into useful voltage. When up to speed, the blades are turned to reduce friction and the skater glides on, conserving power by minimizing unwanted resistance.

Inductors and transformers

AN INDUCTOR IS AN ELECTROMAGNET – a coil of wire, with or without a magnetic core, that produces magnetism when current flows through it. The magnetism forms a store of energy that takes time to fill or empty. So inductors, like capacitors (pp. 20-21), can introduce the time element into electronics. They oppose high-frequency currents, preventing mains voltage disturbances getting into circuits or radio signals getting out. With capacitors, they form electrical resonators that can filter out unwanted signals (pp. 34-35). Modern electronic technology uses inductors sparingly because they are impossible to include in integrated circuits (pp. 52-53). A transformer is two or more coils sharing the same core. It is widely used to step voltages up or down. Changing current through one coil causes magnetic changes that affect all the coils, inducing the same voltage in each turn of wire. Coils with more turns produce more voltage but less current.

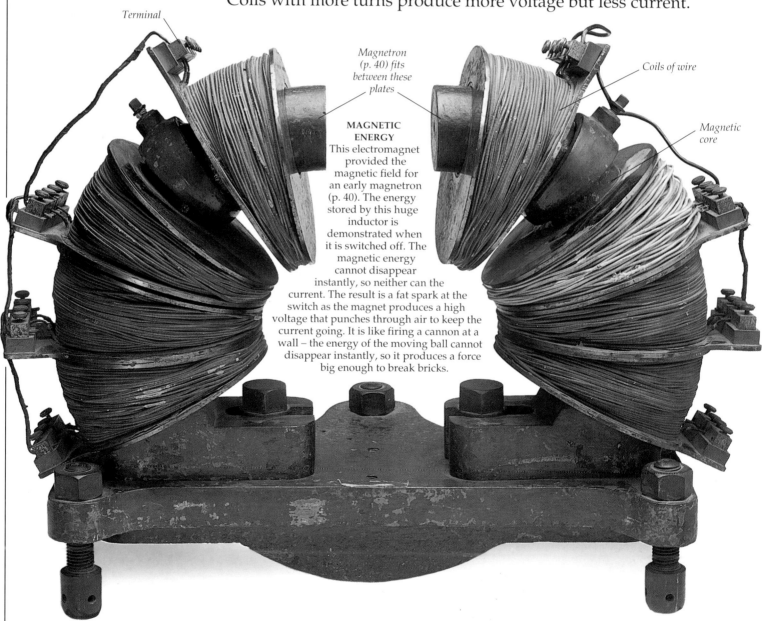

FARADAY'S RING
Michael Faraday discovered in 1831 that starting or stopping the current in one of the wires on this iron ring caused a brief rush of current in the other. The now famous ring is astonishingly like the modern transformer of 160 years later (opposite).

Terminal

Magnetron (p. 40) fits between these plates

Coils of wire

Magnetic core

MAGNETIC ENERGY
This electromagnet provided the magnetic field for an early magnetron (p. 40). The energy stored by this huge inductor is demonstrated when it is switched off. The magnetic energy cannot disappear instantly, so neither can the current. The result is a fat spark at the switch as the magnet produces a high voltage that punches through air to keep the current going. It is like firing a cannon at a wall – the energy of the moving ball cannot disappear instantly, so it produces a force big enough to break bricks.

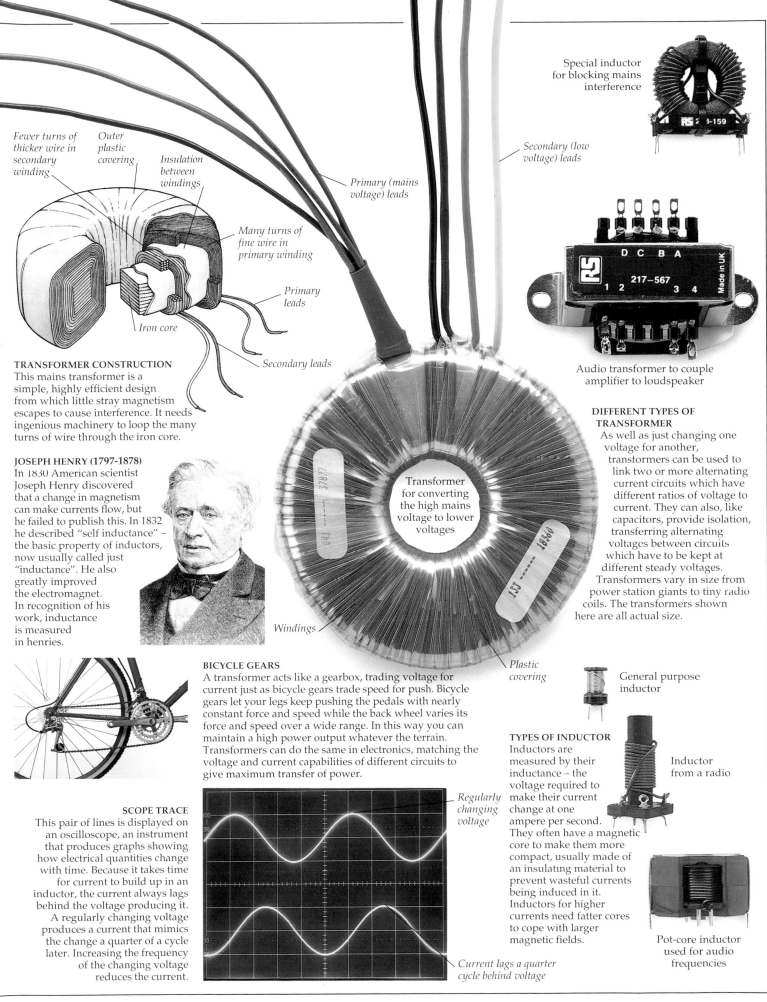

Special inductor
for blocking mains
interference

Fewer turns of thicker wire in secondary winding

Outer plastic covering

Insulation between windings

Many turns of fine wire in primary winding

Primary (mains voltage) leads

Secondary (low voltage) leads

Primary leads

Secondary leads

Iron core

TRANSFORMER CONSTRUCTION
This mains transformer is a simple, highly efficient design from which little stray magnetism escapes to cause interference. It needs ingenious machinery to loop the many turns of wire through the iron core.

JOSEPH HENRY (1797-1878)
In 1830 American scientist Joseph Henry discovered that a change in magnetism can make currents flow, but he failed to publish this. In 1832 he described "self inductance" – the basic property of inductors, now usually called just "inductance". He also greatly improved the electromagnet. In recognition of his work, inductance is measured in henries.

Transformer for converting the high mains voltage to lower voltages

Windings

Audio transformer to couple amplifier to loudspeaker

DIFFERENT TYPES OF TRANSFORMER
As well as just changing one voltage for another, transformers can be used to link two or more alternating current circuits which have different ratios of voltage to current. They can also, like capacitors, provide isolation, transferring alternating voltages between circuits which have to be kept at different steady voltages. Transformers vary in size from power station giants to tiny radio coils. The transformers shown here are all actual size.

BICYCLE GEARS
A transformer acts like a gearbox, trading voltage for current just as bicycle gears trade speed for push. Bicycle gears let your legs keep pushing the pedals with nearly constant force and speed while the back wheel varies its force and speed over a wide range. In this way you can maintain a high power output whatever the terrain. Transformers can do the same in electronics, matching the voltage and current capabilities of different circuits to give maximum transfer of power.

Plastic covering

General purpose inductor

Inductor from a radio

TYPES OF INDUCTOR
Inductors are measured by their inductance – the voltage required to make their current change at one ampere per second. They often have a magnetic core to make them more compact, usually made of an insulating material to prevent wasteful currents being induced in it. Inductors for higher currents need fatter cores to cope with larger magnetic fields.

SCOPE TRACE
This pair of lines is displayed on an oscilloscope, an instrument that produces graphs showing how electrical quantities change with time. Because it takes time for current to build up in an inductor, the current always lags behind the voltage producing it.
   A regularly changing voltage produces a current that mimics the change a quarter of a cycle later. Increasing the frequency of the changing voltage reduces the current.

Regularly changing voltage

Current lags a quarter cycle behind voltage

Pot-core inductor used for audio frequencies

Capacitors

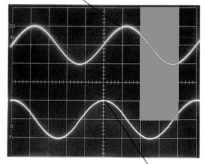

A CAPACITOR IS TWO OR MORE insulated metal plates with every other plate connected to one of two wires. The insulation, usually called the dielectric, prevents a steady current flowing. But connect the capacitor to a battery, and current will flow briefly as electric charge builds up on the plates, stopping only when the increasing capacitor voltage equals the battery voltage. This process takes energy from the battery, which is stored in the dielectric in much the same way as energy is stored in the stretched rubber of a balloon. The way capacitors block steady currents but pass changing ones is often exploited in electronics to isolate parts of a circuit that must be kept at different voltages while enabling signals to travel between them. Capacitors introduce time into electronics, allowing things to happen slowly, or in sequence.

LEYDEN JAR
The capacitor is probably the oldest electronic component. In the 18th century electricity was thought of as a fluid that passed through conductors and could be collected in jars like this. They are really capacitors with metal coatings inside and outside acting as plates and the glass of the jar as the dielectric. The machine shown here produced a high voltage by rubbing a glass disc against cloth pads when the handle was turned. This could charge a nearby jar. In spite of the demise of the fluid theory, capacitors were still called "condensers" until about 1950.

BLOWING UP A BALLOON
You cannot blow through a balloon, but you can blow it up. As it fills, the pressure rises. Eventually, you cannot force in any more air, or the balloon bursts. In the same way, current cannot flow through a capacitor, but can flow into it. The voltage rises, stretching the molecules of the dielectric as electric charge builds up on the plates. The build-up stops when the battery is unable to force in any more charge or, if the voltage is too high, the overstretched dielectric gives way like the rubber of the balloon.

Voltage follows current

Regularly changing current

SCOPE TRACE
Because it takes time for charge to flow into a capacitor, its voltage always lags behind the current producing it. This oscilloscope trace shows how a regularly changing current produces a voltage that mimics the change a quarter of a cycle later. (On the oscilloscope screen, later times are shown towards the right-hand side.)

Capacitor for suppressing interference caused by electric motors

Metallized film capacitor with clear plastic coating

Miniature variable capacitor used for fine tuning inside radio and television sets

Outer plastic coating

Metallized plastic plates

End connector

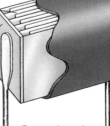

Connecting wire

Construction of metallized film capacitor

DIFFERENT TYPES OF CAPACITOR
Every capacitor is a compromise between size, capacitance (ratio of charge to voltage), high-frequency performance, and maximum working voltage. The metallized film capacitor uses plastic coated with metal, like gift wrap. Many layers are sandwiched together, connected to wires and dipped in plastic. Three types of capacitor are shown here actual size.

ELECTROLYTIC CAPACITOR
Large electrolytic capacitors like this one – shown here about two-thirds its actual size – are used to provide the reserve energy that smooths the current from a large power supply, perhaps in a mainframe computer. For a given volume and working voltage, electrolytic capacitors offer more capacitance than most other types.

Positive connection

Negative connection

Chemically impregnated paper

Aluminium foil

Aluminium can

Plastic insulation

SPACE SAVER
Capacitors with high capacitance can be large. One way to save space is with an electrolytic capacitor, which uses a chemical reaction to create dielectric layers only molecules thick. Because capacitance increases as dielectric thickness decreases, this kind of capacitor can pack a lot of energy into a small volume. The electrolytic capacitor is made by interleaving two strips of foil with paper soaked in a conducting solution, and rolling them up in a can. The dielectric is formed as a thin layer on the surface of one strip by a chemical reaction that takes place when a voltage is applied. If the capacitor is to keep working, this voltage must be maintained at all times.

ELECTRONIC WELCOME
A blizzard of electronically generated light greets the famous every year at the Cannes Film Festival in France. Before electronic flash, photographers used bulbs filled with magnesium wire. Each bulb gave only one flash and had to be changed before the next picture. But, like the electronic flash, the bulbs were often fired by discharging a capacitor.

Flash head

Flash capacitor

FLASH CAMERA
A camera flash works by applying a short burst of high voltage to gas in a glass tube. The electrical energy required is small, but it has to be supplied quickly because the flash is so brief. A battery can neither supply the high voltage, nor deliver energy fast enough, so a capacitor is used instead. An electronic circuit steps up the battery voltage and charges the capacitor. When the button is pressed, the stored energy is released in about one thousandth of a second.

Flexible printed circuit

Lens

Zoom control

See-through modern SLR camera with built-in zoom lens and electronic flash

Building circuits

ALL ELECTRONIC SYSTEMS are made from just a few basic types of components. By themselves, these cannot do anything useful. It is the way they are connected to form circuits that creates the rich variety of electronic technology. Circuit design depends, among other things, on mathematics, much of it worked out in the 19th century. The rules governing the flow of electricity between components were formulated in 1845 by the German scientist Gustav Kirchhoff. Though simple, they are one of the keys to understanding how circuits work. For many basic functions, ready-made circuit designs exist in books or as integrated circuits (pp. 52-53). The designer has to know about these and decide how to link them to perform a given task. When the design is complete, the circuit must be built. Until the 1960s most circuits were put together by hand, with components linked by wires. The development of the printed circuit board – a piece of plastic with holes to accept the components and metal tracks to connect them – means that circuits can now be assembled by machine, greatly reducing the cost of electronic devices.

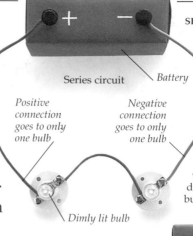

Series circuit

Battery

Positive connection goes to only one bulb

Negative connection goes to only one bulb

Dimly lit bulb

SERIES AND PARALLEL
The same components connected in different ways can behave quite differently. Connected "in series", the battery voltage is split between these bulbs because they act as a potential divider (pp. 16-17). The battery cannot drive much current through each bulb, and they light only dimly. Connected "in parallel", each bulb has the whole of the battery voltage across it, so the battery can drive enough current through each bulb to give a bright light.

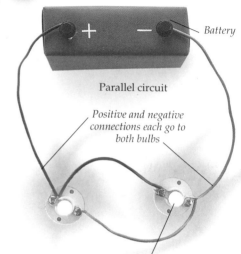

Battery

Parallel circuit

Positive and negative connections each go to both bulbs

Brightly lit bulb

CIRCUIT LAWS
The German physicist Gustav Kirchhoff (1824-1887) extended Ohm's law (pp. 16-17) to deal with situations where more than one resistor was connected to more than one battery. His circuit laws state that all the current flowing into any point must also flow out of it, and that the total voltage driving current around any loop must equal the total of the voltages opposing it. These simple principles allow complicated circuits to be analyzed mathematically and are used by computer programs that help in circuit design.

Tuning capacitor

Speaker

Tuning knob

Valve

Side view of Sargrove radio

SARGROVE RADIO (1940S)
John Sargrove (1906-1974) was a British engineer who in the 1940s built machines that could make not just printed circuit boards, but complete radios like this one. His machines sprayed plastic blanks with metal to form circuits including resistors, inductors, and capacitors. They even attached large components like valve holders. Only valve insertion and final adjustment needed human hands. His ideas were sound, but his machines were thought to threaten jobs.

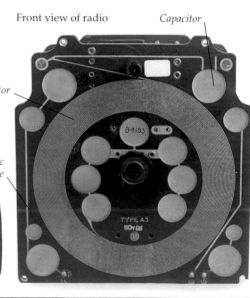

Front view of radio

Capacitor

Inductor

Plastic plate

AC CIRCUIT

Most electronic circuits carry voltages and currents that continually reverse their direction. They are called "alternating current" (AC) circuits. Inductors and capacitors respond to AC in different ways. At low frequencies, the inductor offers little opposition to the current, so only a small voltage appears across it, while the capacitor opposes the current more strongly, producing a higher voltage. The situation is reversed at high frequencies. The voltages across inductor and capacitor are in opposite directions. At just one frequency – the "resonant" frequency – they will cancel out, allowing large currents to flow. This effect is used in filters (pp. 34-35).

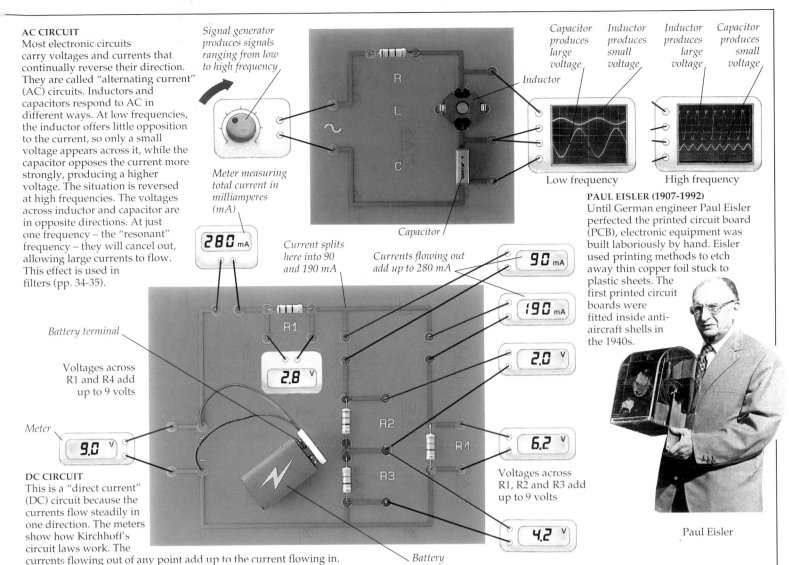

Signal generator produces signals ranging from low to high frequency

Meter measuring total current in milliamperes (mA)

280 mA

Capacitor produces large voltage *Inductor produces small voltage* *Inductor produces large voltage* *Capacitor produces small voltage*

Inductor

Low frequency   High frequency

Capacitor

Current splits here into 90 and 190 mA

Currents flowing out add up to 280 mA

90 mA
190 mA
2.0 V

Battery terminal

2.8 V

R1

Voltages across R1 and R4 add up to 9 volts

Meter

9.0 V

R2

R4

6.2 V

R3

Voltages across R1, R2 and R3 add up to 9 volts

4.2 V

Battery

PAUL EISLER (1907-1992)

Until German engineer Paul Eisler perfected the printed circuit board (PCB), electronic equipment was built laboriously by hand. Eisler used printing methods to etch away thin copper foil stuck to plastic sheets. The first printed circuit boards were fitted inside anti-aircraft shells in the 1940s.

Paul Eisler

DC CIRCUIT

This is a "direct current" (DC) circuit because the currents flow steadily in one direction. The meters show how Kirchhoff's circuit laws work. The currents flowing out of any point add up to the current flowing in. The voltages around any path between the battery terminals add up to the battery voltage. The actual voltages and currents depend on the resistor values and are given by Ohm's law.

Tracks connecting components

PRINTED CIRCUIT BOARD

Printed circuit boards, like this one from a small computer, are made from plastic coated with copper foil. The foil is etched away to leave tracks that connect the components together. A layer of lacquer protects the board except where components are inserted. This allows the components to be fixed in place by skimming the entire board across a bath of molten solder. More elaborate boards have several layers of tracks.

THE LANGUAGE OF ELECTRONICS

Electronics engineers use special units to measure both electricity and the properties of components. They also use a visual language in which every component has a standard symbol. These symbols can be linked to form diagrams showing exactly how a circuit is made.

BASIC UNITS

A = ampere (unit of current)
V = volt (unit of voltage)
W = watt (unit of power)
Ω = ohm (unit of resistance)
H = henry (unit of inductance)
F = farad (unit of capacitance)
Hz = hertz (unit of frequency)

PREFIXES TO INDICATE FRACTIONS OR MULTIPLES OF UNITS

p = pico (1 trillionth)
n = nano (1 billionth)
µ = micro (1 millionth)
m = milli (1 thousandth)
k = kilo (1 thousand)
M = mega (1 million)
G = giga (1 billion)

CIRCUIT SYMBOLS

battery
resistor
potentiometer
inductor
transformer
capacitor
pre-set capacitor
electrolytic capacitor
diode
light-emitting diode
bipolar transistor
field effect transistor

Communicating with electricity

THE DISCOVERIES OF OERSTED and Faraday (pp. 10-11) led to significant changes in people's lives. A telegraph message travelled 100 million times faster than a horse or ship, enabling nations to trade efficiently over vast areas of the globe. Electric light was brighter and cheaper than gas, extending the day for work and leisure. But the biggest effect was to give people the power of information. Railways used the telegraph to aid smooth running and distributed newspapers carrying reports telegraphed from all over the world. Some of the effects of electrical science seemed simply magical. The theoretical work of British mathematician James Clerk Maxwell (1831-1879) and German physicist Heinrich Hertz (1857-1894) led, by 1900, to communication with ships on the high seas. All of this was accomplished with only the crudest means of amplifying and detecting the faltering signals that crossed oceans and continents.

SIMPLE COMMUNICATION
The first electric telegraphs all used more than one wire. It was American portrait painter Samuel F. B. Morse (1791-1872) who realized that, given a suitable code tapped out by key, a single wire could carry any message.

Receiving dial

Transmitting dial | *Handle turns generator inside* | *Terminal*

Transmit/receive switch

Letter button

SIEMENS GALVANOMETER
Magnetized needle — *Terminal*
Rain and storm damage caused electricity to leak away from telegraph wires and also produced bad contacts. Galvanometers like this one, made in about 1890, were used to find faults by comparing the currents in two similar wires. A large difference indicated that there was a problem. Inside the apparatus a magnetized needle is suspended over a pair of coils – one coil for each wire. The terminals are connected to the telegraph wires being tested.

TELEGRAPHY ON THE BATTLE FIELD
In 1864, near the end of the American Civil War, Ulysses S. Grant (1822-1885) took command of the Union army. By using the telegraph to keep in contact with his far-flung troops, he defeated the Confederate army. Grant realized that the telegraph could provide him with vital information.

PORTABLE ABC TELEGRAPH
British musical instrument maker and professor of experimental philosophy Sir Charles Wheatstone (1802-1875) always tried hard to make his electric telegraphs as easy to use as possible. This ABC telegraph of 1858 was so simple an operator could use it after a few minutes' training. To transmit a message, the handle was turned and the buttons pressed. A generator inside created electrical impulses that made a similar needle at the receiving end rotate in step, pausing at the letters of the message.

BUSINESS VENTURES
The telephone made business communications between companies in different countries much quicker. The first telephone link between London and Paris was opened with much ceremony in 1891.

ALEXANDER GRAHAM BELL
Bell (1847-1922) was a Scot who taught the deaf in the USA. In 1876 he devised the first successful telephone, using magnetism and electricity to produce a simple, reliable system. The telephone was the first really easy-to-use device for communicating at a distance.

EDISON TELEPHONE
This strange-looking telephone was designed by Thomas Edison (1847-1931) because he needed to avoid using the transmitter and receiver already patented by Bell in 1876. Edison's transmitter was effective, but his receiver was too inconvenient to survive.

Drum inside receiver is sensitive to incoming currents

Bell to signal incoming call

Handle turns drum

Transmitter uses varying resistance of carbon to send speech

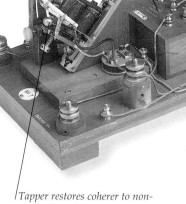

Aerial transformer to increase efficiency

Battery supplies current to operate the relay

Relay links the signal and the circuit

Coherer

Tapper restores coherer to non-conducting state

MARCONI RECEIVER
This 1899 receiver by Italian inventor Guglielmo Marconi (1874-1937) detects messages sent as bursts of radio waves. With this equipment, the messages can be treated as if they had come by wire. The vital component is the coherer – a device that conducts electricity only when subjected to radio waves. The receiver uses an electromagnetic relay to convert the small coherer current into a large telegraph current.

Transmitter varies current as pencil moves

Clockwork to drive rollers

COWPER'S WRITING TELEGRAPH
"Telegraph" comes from two Greek words meaning "writing at a distance". In 1878 British engineer William Cowper (1819-1893) took this literally and designed a machine that could reproduce a message being written by someone many kilometres away. Although working on a completely different principle, it was a distant (and unsuccessful) cousin of today's fax machine (pp. 60-61).

Paper tape

Rollers

Rollers pull tape through machine

Handwritten message reproduced at distant receiver

Pencil connected to motion transmitters

Moving electrons

Everything around us is made of atoms. Atoms themselves are made of still smaller particles called protons, neutrons and electrons. Electrons are the tiniest of these particles. Each one of them carries the smallest possible amount of negative electricity, and even tiny bits of matter contain billions of them. In most materials, and especially in good insulators like glass or plastics, electrons are held firmly in place by the heavier, positively charged protons. But some materials, mostly metals, contain electrons that have enough energy to roam about. This allows the electrons to transport electricity from one place to another, and means that metals are good conductors. They are used for this purpose in all electrical systems. And when metals are heated, this gives their electrons still more energy, sometimes enough to break free completely, like rockets escaping the pull of the Earth.

NAMING THE ELECTRON
In 1897 the British physicist J. J. Thomson (1856-1940) found that he could use many different materials to obtain negatively charged particles with exactly the same properties. He called these particles "electrons". For his experiments he used a glass tube with metal plates inside it and with most of the air pumped out. It was called a cathode ray tube and had been developed by scientists investigating the effect of electricity on gases.

Vacuum

Electrons holding metal together

Mobile electron

Proton

Cool metal

Free electron

Proton

Mobile electron

Heated metal

ELECTRON STRUCTURE OF METALS
Although metals contain plenty of mobile electrons, very few of the electrons have enough energy at normal temperatures to break free from the electrical attraction that holds them inside the material. Heating metals up to quite modest temperatures – cooler than the filament of a light bulb – makes a big difference to the energy of their electrons, so that many of them can escape into space. Once free, preferably in a vacuum where there is nothing to bump into, they can be guided by electricity or magnetism to form a controlled electric current. This is the basic principle of the valve (pp. 28-29), once the backbone of electronics, and the cathode ray tube, which is still the best way of showing television pictures.

ELECTRONIC CHARGE
Robert Millikan (1868-1953) was an American physicist who deduced the actual charge of the electron in 1911. He did this by measuring the electric charge of an oil droplet.

Picture amplifier

HEAD AMPLIFIER A 1207

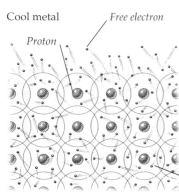

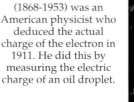

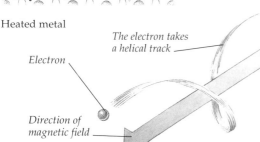

Electron

The electron takes a helical track

Direction of magnetic field

THE PATH OF A MOVING ELECTRON
A moving electron constitutes an electric current, and so creates a magnetic field (pp. 10-11). Another magnetic field can interact with this, producing a path varying from a tight coil, used in a magnetron (p. 40), to a straight line, used in a high-power klystron (p. 41).

AURORA BOREALIS
These spectacular night-sky displays are seen near the Earth's poles. They happen when electrons and protons, ejected by the Sun, hit the upper atmosphere and are trapped in the Earth's magnetic field.

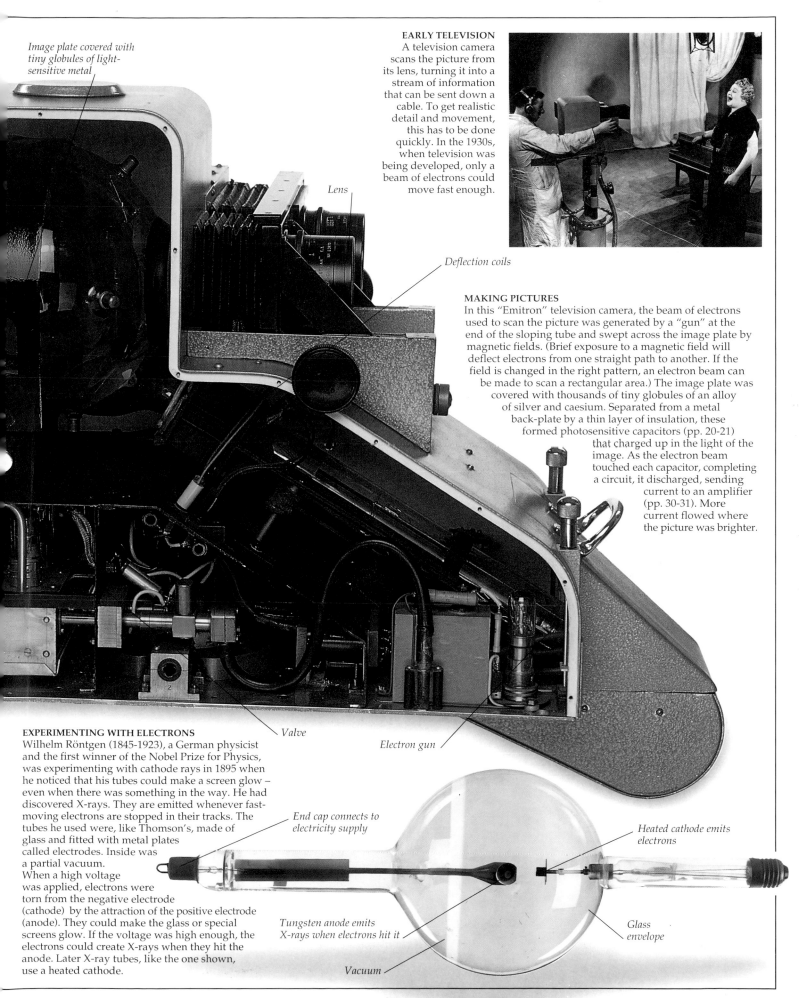

Image plate covered with tiny globules of light-sensitive metal

EARLY TELEVISION
A television camera scans the picture from its lens, turning it into a stream of information that can be sent down a cable. To get realistic detail and movement, this has to be done quickly. In the 1930s, when television was being developed, only a beam of electrons could move fast enough.

Lens

Deflection coils

MAKING PICTURES
In this "Emitron" television camera, the beam of electrons used to scan the picture was generated by a "gun" at the end of the sloping tube and swept across the image plate by magnetic fields. (Brief exposure to a magnetic field will deflect electrons from one straight path to another. If the field is changed in the right pattern, an electron beam can be made to scan a rectangular area.) The image plate was covered with thousands of tiny globules of an alloy of silver and caesium. Separated from a metal back-plate by a thin layer of insulation, these formed photosensitive capacitors (pp. 20-21) that charged up in the light of the image. As the electron beam touched each capacitor, completing a circuit, it discharged, sending current to an amplifier (pp. 30-31). More current flowed where the picture was brighter.

Valve

Electron gun

EXPERIMENTING WITH ELECTRONS
Wilhelm Röntgen (1845-1923), a German physicist and the first winner of the Nobel Prize for Physics, was experimenting with cathode rays in 1895 when he noticed that his tubes could make a screen glow – even when there was something in the way. He had discovered X-rays. They are emitted whenever fast-moving electrons are stopped in their tracks. The tubes he used were, like Thomson's, made of glass and fitted with metal plates called electrodes. Inside was a partial vacuum. When a high voltage was applied, electrons were torn from the negative electrode (cathode) by the attraction of the positive electrode (anode). They could make the glass or special screens glow. If the voltage was high enough, the electrons could create X-rays when they hit the anode. Later X-ray tubes, like the one shown, use a heated cathode.

End cap connects to electricity supply

Heated cathode emits electrons

Tungsten anode emits X-rays when electrons hit it

Glass envelope

Vacuum

27

Using electrons

IT TOOK EXPERIMENTERS nearly 30 years to realize that electrons given off by hot metals could be used to amplify signals. Thomas Edison suspected as early as 1880 that something was travelling through the vacuum inside his light bulbs. In 1904 Ambrose Fleming used this "Edison effect" to make a diode – a device with two electrodes that, because it conducted electricity one way only, he called a valve. It could detect weak radio waves by turning their alternating current into direct current (p. 23) that worked an indicator, but could not increase their power. When Lee De Forest added a third electrode, creating the triode, it became possible to convert a weak signal into a stronger one. The triode was the first true amplifier.

MINIATURE VALVE
Small glass-based valves like this appeared in the 1940s. They were the most common type in use when valves began to be replaced by transistors in the late 1950s (pp. 38-39).

FLEMING EXPERIMENTAL BULB
John Ambrose Fleming (1849-1945), a British professor of electrical engineering, investigated Edison's light bulbs in 1889 (see below). He used bulbs like this with an extra wire electrode inside. Fleming remembered them in 1904 while seeking a detector for radio waves. He realized that electrons from the filament could only flow one way, because they would be repelled if the wire became more negative than the filament. This led to his "oscillation valve", which acted on oscillating radio currents like the one-way valve of a tyre, turning them into steady current to work a telegraph.

Wire to plate

Wire to grid

Plate

Grid

Vacuum

Glass bulb

Vacuum

Filament

Negative filament connection through retaining screw

Positive filament connection through end contact

Carbon filament

Connection to anode

Anode

AUDION VALVE
Invented by Lee De Forest in 1906, this Audion valve of 1907 was adapted from a car headlamp bulb. The crucial difference from Fleming's earlier valves was an extra wire or "grid" positioned in the path of the electrons. This could control them, making amplification possible. With three electrodes (filament, grid and plate), the Audion is a triode. Its primitive design meant that it hardly amplified at all, but it was a sensitive radio detector.

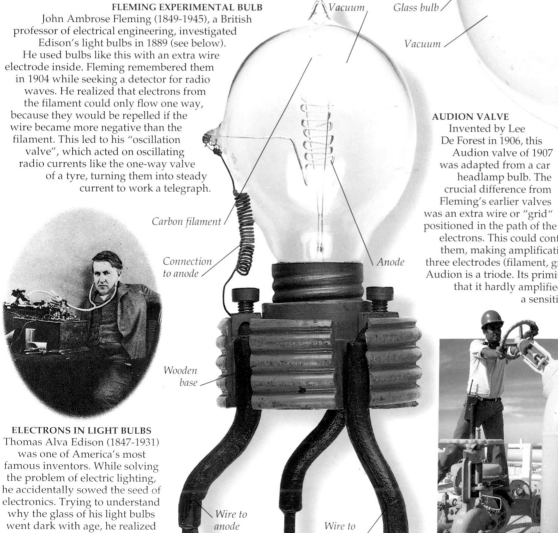

Wooden base

ELECTRONS IN LIGHT BULBS
Thomas Alva Edison (1847-1931) was one of America's most famous inventors. While solving the problem of electric lighting, he accidentally sowed the seed of electronics. Trying to understand why the glass of his light bulbs went dark with age, he realized that something was travelling from the negative to the positive side of the filaments.

Wire to anode

Wire to filament

VALVE IN A PIPELINE
Valves work much like a valve in an oil pipe. Pressure in the pipe forces the oil one way. By adjusting the position of a gate inside the pipe, as here on a Libyan desert pipeline, the flow can be controlled. In a similar way, electrons attracted from negative cathode to positive anode are controlled by the voltage of the grid in between.

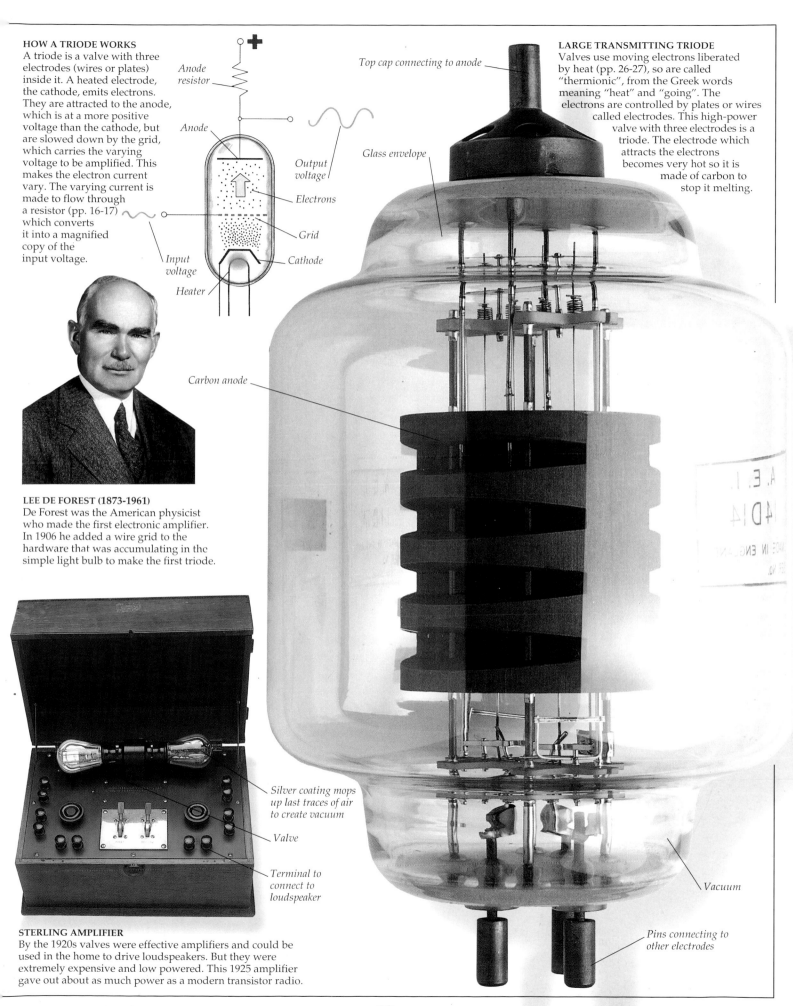

HOW A TRIODE WORKS

A triode is a valve with three electrodes (wires or plates) inside it. A heated electrode, the cathode, emits electrons. They are attracted to the anode, which is at a more positive voltage than the cathode, but are slowed down by the grid, which carries the varying voltage to be amplified. This makes the electron current vary. The varying current is made to flow through a resistor (pp. 16-17) which converts it into a magnified copy of the input voltage.

Anode resistor

Anode

Output voltage

Electrons

Grid

Cathode

Input voltage

Heater

LEE DE FOREST (1873-1961)

De Forest was the American physicist who made the first electronic amplifier. In 1906 he added a wire grid to the hardware that was accumulating in the simple light bulb to make the first triode.

STERLING AMPLIFIER

By the 1920s valves were effective amplifiers and could be used in the home to drive loudspeakers. But they were extremely expensive and low powered. This 1925 amplifier gave out about as much power as a modern transistor radio.

Silver coating mops up last traces of air to create vacuum

Valve

Terminal to connect to loudspeaker

LARGE TRANSMITTING TRIODE

Valves use moving electrons liberated by heat (pp. 26-27), so are called "thermionic", from the Greek words meaning "heat" and "going". The electrons are controlled by plates or wires called electrodes. This high-power valve with three electrodes is a triode. The electrode which attracts the electrons becomes very hot so it is made of carbon to stop it melting.

Top cap connecting to anode

Glass envelope

Carbon anode

Vacuum

Pins connecting to other electrodes

Amplifiers

AMPLIFIERS TURN WEAK ELECTRICAL SIGNALS into stronger ones. They allow a small amount of power, representing information, to control a much larger amount of power that can do useful work. In this way amplifiers make the vital link between information and energy. Making valves or transistors amplify requires care if their output is not to be a distorted version of their input. In 1927 Harold Black solved this problem with his idea of "negative feedback" in which an amplifier monitors and corrects its own errors. Feedback of another kind can turn an amplifier into an oscillator (p. 33). And if an amplifier is driven hard enough, so that its output is forced to one extreme or the other, it can act as an electrically controlled switch. Computers contain huge assemblies of such switches. In these machines, information controls not just energy but more information, demonstrating the might of the amplifier.

USING A MEGAPHONE ON THE FILM SET
An amplifier is not just anything that makes things bigger or louder. A true amplifier turns raw power into controlled power. The megaphone makes sounds louder, but is not an amplifier, because all it does is use the existing power of the voice more efficiently.

A HOMELY AMP
An amplifier is essential for family listening. Without one, headphones must be used, as radio circuits do not give enough power to work a loudspeaker. The low-powered amplifier in this 1940s radio entertained the children without annoying the neighbours.

6VLT. BATT.

No 1907

S.G.BROWN'S
TELEPHONE RELAY
ACTON
LONDON W.

LE 500°

Capsule of carbon changes resistance when vibrated

AUDIO AMPLIFIER
Early radios produced little power, so extra amplifiers were often added. There was no industry producing them on a large scale, but they could always be built at home, like this magnificent creation of the late 1920s. Big amplifiers need plenty of raw power to work on, and this one had a hefty power supply. It also used two valves to drive the loudspeaker (pp. 42-43), one pushing, the other pulling. A similar arrangement is still used in modern amplifiers.

BROWN REPEATER
Amplifying a continuously varying signal like a telephone call was difficult without electronics, but not impossible. The Brown repeater of 1918 was installed at telephone exchanges to boost long-distance calls. It exploited the amplifying ability of the carbon granule microphone also used in telephones (p. 25). It contains one of these microphones pressed against an iron reed that reproduces the sound of the call to be amplified. It produced severe distortion.

Terminal

Coils to energize magnet

Coils for incoming telephone currents

Delicate steel reed vibrates in magnetic field

Radio signal input 0.000000001 W

Intermediate output 0.01W

Heat 2 W *Heat 2 W*

Audio output 2 W

Heat 1.95 W

Intermediate frequency amplifier
2 W

Audio amplifier
4 W

Actual sound output 0.05 W

Power supply

Heat 2 W

Loudspeaker

Power input 8W

RADIO POWER FLOWS
A radio uses a chain of amplifiers to feed power from the wall socket, under the control of an incredibly small amount of power from the aerial, to the speaker. Nearly all of it is wasted as heat, but because ears are very sensitive it still sounds loud.

1962-96 PT.

Capacitor
smooths
supply
voltage

Low
power
valve
tube

Mains transformer
changes mains
voltage to suit
amplifier

Large inductor

Variable
resistor

High-power
valves drive
loudspeaker

Rectifier valve
converts AC
mains to DC for
valves

HAROLD S. BLACK (1898-1983)
In 1927 Harold S. Black was working at the
Bell telephone laboratories in the USA trying
to design amplifiers that would not distort
signals. He realized that subtracting a little of
an amplifier's output from its input, while
reducing its amplification, would also reduce the
distortion. Simple mathematics proved that this
"negative feedback" could make a bad amplifier
into a good one. It has been used ever since.

Output
transformer
delivers
power in
form
suited to
loudspeaker

Power relay

Operational
amplifier

Audio amplifier

**AMPLIFYING
COMPONENTS**
Although not a true
amplifier, the relay can be
used to switch heavy
currents or, in a smaller
version, to connect and
disconnect signals.
Amplifiers available as
integrated circuits
(pp. 52-53) can perform
many functions. The
audio amplifier can
deliver over 20 watts
to a suitable speaker.
Operational
amplifiers have a
wide range of uses
in low-power
analogue circuits.
The components
above are shown
actual size.

Volume control

31

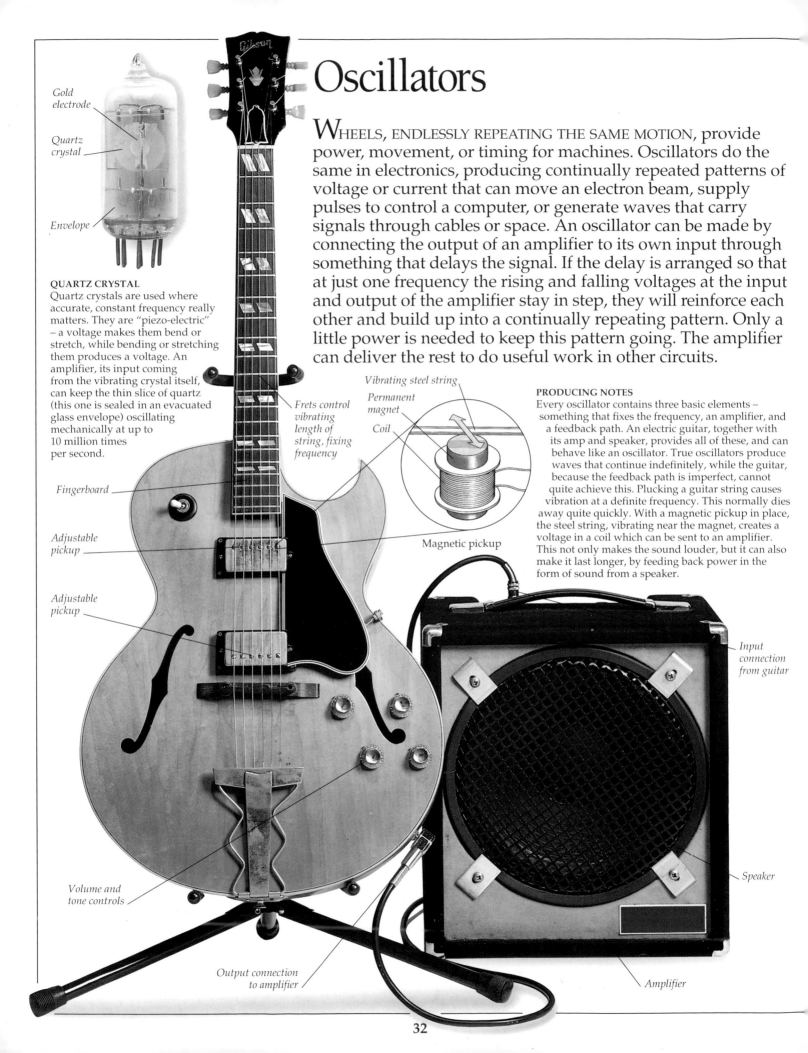

Oscillators

W‍HEELS, ENDLESSLY REPEATING THE SAME MOTION, provide power, movement, or timing for machines. Oscillators do the same in electronics, producing continually repeated patterns of voltage or current that can move an electron beam, supply pulses to control a computer, or generate waves that carry signals through cables or space. An oscillator can be made by connecting the output of an amplifier to its own input through something that delays the signal. If the delay is arranged so that at just one frequency the rising and falling voltages at the input and output of the amplifier stay in step, they will reinforce each other and build up into a continually repeating pattern. Only a little power is needed to keep this pattern going. The amplifier can deliver the rest to do useful work in other circuits.

Gold electrode

Quartz crystal

Envelope

QUARTZ CRYSTAL
Quartz crystals are used where accurate, constant frequency really matters. They are "piezo-electric" – a voltage makes them bend or stretch, while bending or stretching them produces a voltage. An amplifier, its input coming from the vibrating crystal itself, can keep the thin slice of quartz (this one is sealed in an evacuated glass envelope) oscillating mechanically at up to 10 million times per second.

Fingerboard

Adjustable pickup

Adjustable pickup

Volume and tone controls

Frets control vibrating length of string, fixing frequency

Vibrating steel string

Permanent magnet

Coil

Magnetic pickup

PRODUCING NOTES
Every oscillator contains three basic elements – something that fixes the frequency, an amplifier, and a feedback path. An electric guitar, together with its amp and speaker, provides all of these, and can behave like an oscillator. True oscillators produce waves that continue indefinitely, while the guitar, because the feedback path is imperfect, cannot quite achieve this. Plucking a guitar string causes vibration at a definite frequency. This normally dies away quite quickly. With a magnetic pickup in place, the steel string, vibrating near the magnet, creates a voltage in a coil which can be sent to an amplifier. This not only makes the sound louder, but it can also make it last longer, by feeding back power in the form of sound from a speaker.

Input connection from guitar

Speaker

Output connection to amplifier

Amplifier

Types of oscillator

There are two basic kinds of oscillator. Both need amplifiers, but the frequency is fixed in different ways. Relaxation oscillators accumulate energy until it causes a switch (a kind of amplifier) to operate, dumping the energy and starting the cycle again. Their frequency is not very constant. Harmonic oscillators accumulate energy in one form at the expense of another, then swap it back. An amplifier replaces any energy lost. Although it produces waves of only one shape, this kind of oscillator is accurate and widely used in electronics.

WATER SCARECROW IN THE GARDEN
Water at a height stores energy. As the bucket of this mechanical relaxation oscillator fills, it gets heavier and overbalances, dumping its energy with the water (and scaring any stray animals in the garden). It can then swing back and fill again. The frequency is fixed by the time this takes. An electronic equivalent is a capacitor slowly charging up until it operates a switch that quickly discharges it.

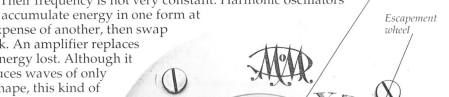

Balance wheel

Escapement wheel

Hairspring

Cathode ray tube

CLOCK ESCAPEMENT
This mechanical harmonic oscillator – the escapement mechanism in a clock – stores energy as motion of the wheel and as strain in the spring. Energy swaps between the two as the wheel speeds and slows and the spring coils and uncoils. The escapement acts as an amplifier, feeding in energy from the clock. The frequency is fixed by the stiffness of the spring and the mass and shape of the wheel. The electronic equivalent is a capacitor and inductor connected together, swapping electric and magnetic energy in a similar way to produce high-frequency oscillations.

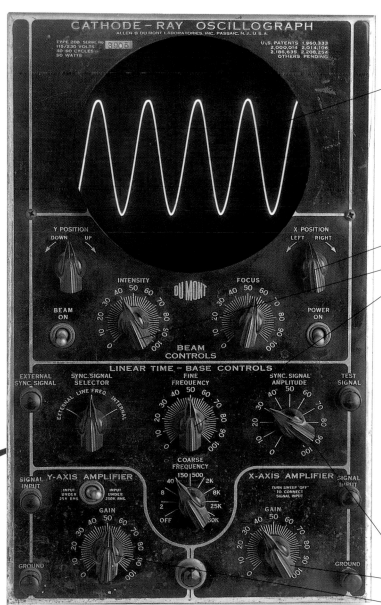

Position control

Brightness control

Control for internal sweep oscillator frequency

OSCILLOSCOPE
Seeing the waves made by oscillators was difficult until German scientist Ferdinand Braun (1850-1918) invented a form of cathode ray oscilloscope in 1897. This one was made around 1945. An internal oscillator repeatedly sweeps a beam of electrons across the screen at constant speed. The input voltage moves the beam up and down, drawing a picture of the wave. Modern oscilloscopes often display the picture digitally, sometimes on a computer screen (pp. 56-57).

Synchronization control gives steady picture

Width control

Height control

ANIMAL TRACKER
Scientists can study the behaviour of penguins in the Antarctic by fitting them with a radio tracking device. This is a combined harmonic and relaxation oscillator that transmits in short bursts, saving the battery. Using a directional aerial, researchers can follow the "bleeps" and map the birds' movements.

How filters work

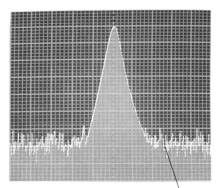

SIEVING ACCORDING TO SIZE
A garden sieve is similar to a "low-pass" filter in electronics. It allows everything below a certain size to get through. What is left behind in the sieve has been "high-pass" filtered – it consists of everything above a certain size.

FILTERS ARE FAMILIAR IN EVERYDAY LIFE. In the kitchen or garden they sort things by size. In electronics, filters almost always respond to the frequency of signals (pp. 14-15), passing low, high, or a chosen band of frequencies, and blocking others. Filters are needed because real signals contain a mixture of frequencies, not all of them useful. A radio aerial, for example, picks up a multitude of stations, but a filter ensures that only one gets through. Other filters block everything above a given frequency, maybe to reduce "hiss" on old tapes. Low frequencies can be blocked too, perhaps to remove the "rumble" produced by an old record player. Filters can use either analogue or digital techniques (pp. 46-47). Analogue filters have been used since the 19th century. They rely on the way inductors and capacitors respond to different frequencies. Digital filters use fast microprocessors (pp. 58-59) to transform the signal mathematically into one without the unwanted frequencies.

FUEL GAUGE
The fuel gauge in a car responds to the level of liquid in the tank. The level varies wildly as the car goes over bumps, but the reading remains steady because it is low-pass filtered to remove rapid changes. This can be seen when the car is first switched on – the fuel reading takes several seconds to reach its true value.

Filter response has wide skirts that let unwanted signals through

INEFFICIENT BAND-PASS FILTER
"Band-pass" filters block both low and high frequencies and allow through a chosen band only. This trace shows how a poor-quality filter, using an inductor which absorbs signal energy, can produce wide "skirts" that let unwanted signals through as well as the chosen band.

NARROW FILTER
Careful design of a simple band-pass filter, using an inductor and a capacitor resonating at the centre of the band, can give good rejection of unwanted frequencies. But the shape of the filter's response means that some wanted frequencies will be rejected too.

Unwanted frequencies reduced

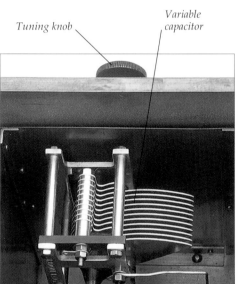

Tuning knob

Variable capacitor

Fixed inductor

Valve

EARLY RADIO TUNED CIRCUIT (left)
Until the 1980s rejection of unwanted radio stations was partly done by components like this. A fixed inductor is used with a variable capacitor – connected to the tuning knob – to form a variable band-pass filter that can be tuned to the frequency of the wanted station. In this home-built receiver of the late 1920s the signal passes through several such filters, each of which has to be separately tuned by hand.

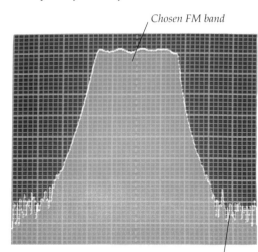

Chosen FM band

FM FILTER
Simple filters are not good enough for an FM radio signal, with its very wide spectrum (p. 49). Filters using several resonators tuned to different frequencies can produce a response which, as this spectrum analyzer image shows, is reasonably "flat" while giving good rejection outside the wanted band. The resonators are often quartz crystals or ceramic plates.

Rejected frequencies

MECHANICAL FILTER

Some types of filter can absorb most of the signal's unwanted energy. The springs and shock absorbers in the forks of this bike form a mechanical low-pass filter that transforms destructive energy, released as the bike hits the ground, into harmless heat. The filter partially isolates the rider from the vertical motion of the wheels, making the ride just a little less uncomfortable.

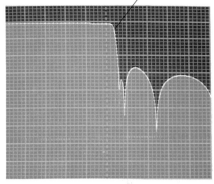

Absorbent plastic prevents waves reflecting back

Comb of electrodes makes quartz ripple at one wavelength

Metal package

Quartz plate

Connecting wire

A COMPONENT FOR RADAR AND TELEVISION

The properties of travelling waves (pp. 12-13) can be used in filters. Structures in their path can block some wavelengths while helping others on their way. Electromagnetic waves travel so fast that these structures might need to be very large. By converting the waves to much slower ripples on the surface of a quartz plate, compact and effective "surface acoustic wave" (SAW) filters for radar and television can be made.

HIGH- AND LOW-PASS FILTERS

Filters are never perfect. These two displays show that instead of unwanted frequencies being completely blocked, a little of their power creeps through. As with all filters there is also a region where signals are neither totally blocked nor totally passed. (On the spectrum analyzer screen, higher frequencies are shown towards the right-hand side.)

TUNING A RADIO

Modern radios use a variable filter followed by a fixed-frequency filter. To select a particular station, its frequency is changed to the filter's fixed frequency by mixing the signal with one generated by a variable-frequency oscillator (pp. 32-33). When the tuning knob is turned, the variable filter tunes to the wanted station, while the oscillator adjusts its frequency to shift the station into the band passed by the fixed filter.

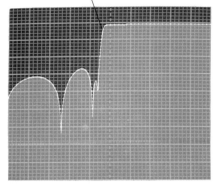

Cut-off frequency

Cut-off frequency

A high-pass filter lets through frequencies above its "cut-off" frequency

A low-pass filter mirrors the high-pass filter, letting through only low frequencies

"Magic eye" shows maximum light when tuning is correct

Tuning scale indicates frequency

FM selector button

Tuning knob

Semiconductors

SEMICONDUCTORS ARE THE KEY to modern electronics. These materials are electrical conductors which are nearly insulators. Unlike metals, only a few of their electrons roam free, while others hop from atom to atom, leaving "holes" which act like positive charges moving the opposite way. Adding impurities to semiconductors, a process called doping, changes the way they conduct, allowing solid structures to be created in which electrons can be controlled electrically. Silicon is a semiconductor that has been used in components since the earliest days of radio. It is now the mainstay of electronics. In the early 1940s, however, it was the rare element germanium that seemed more promising for better radar detectors. By 1945 it was being used in attempts to make a semiconductor device that would amplify (pp. 38-39).

CRYSTAL SET
The crystal set, popular in the 1920s, was called after the semiconductor crystal that it used. By twiddling a fine wire – the "cat's whisker" – you could find a spot on the crystal where a one-way current would pass, allowing the sound signal carried by the radio waves to operate the headphones. In the 1940s scientists started trying to understand how devices like this, developed by trial and error, really worked. This eventually led to a huge expansion of the semiconductor industry.

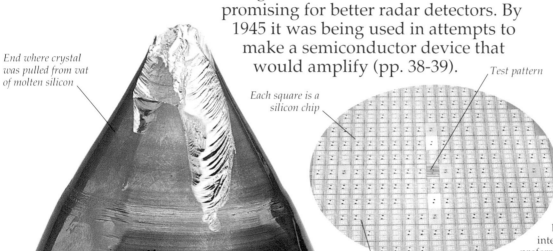

End where crystal was pulled from vat of molten silicon

Each square is a silicon chip

Test pattern

Diamond-tipped saw separates chips along cutting line

SILICON WAFER
Slicing and polishing a large semiconductor crystal yields thin discs or "wafers" on which microscopic electronic components can be created by selective doping, forming integrated circuits (pp. 52-53). Silicon is preferred because it is cheap and strong.

SILICON CRYSTAL
Silicon is by far the most widely used semiconductor. Like its earlier rival germanium, silicon atoms have four outer electrons, but unlike germanium, silicon is not rare. After oxygen it is the second most abundant element on Earth. Its electrons are less mobile than those of germanium, but it is also less temperature sensitive. Large crystals like this are formed by pulling them slowly out of a vat of molten material.

Silicon

Gold mount

SILICON LOCKET
The properties of silicon have been known for nearly a century. This chunk was originally part of a radio detector, but is now mounted as a piece of jewellery. It was used in 1910 on the first British cargo ship to carry radio, the SS *Nonsuch*.

Body of crystal

A BOUNTEOUS MATERIAL
The starting point for microchips is sand, a compound of silicon and oxygen. By melting sand with other materials, the silicon can be extracted, but making a crystal good enough for chips needs repeated refining until impurities are down to less than one atom in a billion.

SEMICONDUCTOR ELEMENTS

When the Russian chemist Dmitri Mendeleyev (1834-1907) listed the elements in order of atomic weight, he found that elements with similar properties appeared at regular intervals. He constructed a table in which related elements appear in vertical groups. Gaps in this table allowed him to predict properties of undiscovered elements. One, in a gap below silicon, he called "ekasilicon". This semiconductor was found in 1886 by the German chemist Clemens Winkler (1838-1904). He named it germanium, after his country.

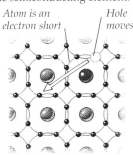

Semiconductors

THE PERIODIC TABLE

Most of the elements in the periodic table are metals. About 20 on the right of the table are non-metals. The semiconducting elements lie between. Some are only semiconducting in a particular state. There are also many semiconducting compounds that are made up of more than one semiconducting element.

Cathode lead

DOPING SEMICONDUCTORS

"Intrinsic" silicon conducts slightly because a few electrons have enough energy to escape from their atoms. Others hop into the resulting holes, leaving new holes behind. The electrons and the moving holes each carry half the current. Adding a proportion of atoms with five outer electrons increases the number of electrons and reduces the number of holes, giving "n-type" silicon, a better conductor in which electrons carry most of the current. Adding atoms with only three outer electrons reduces the number of electrons, but increases the number of holes, forming "p-type" silicon in which holes carry most of the current.

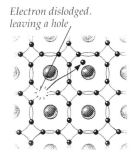

Electron dislodged, leaving a hole

Intrinsic semiconductor

Impurity atom

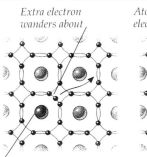

Extra electron wanders about

n-type semiconductor

Atom is an electron short

Hole moves

p-type semiconductor

SMALL AND QUICK

This tiny silicon diode is useful for controlling signals. Its small size means that it can work at high frequencies.

SILICON DIODE

A silicon crystal with adjoining p- and n-type regions forms a diode, a device that conducts electricity in one direction only. Holes leak out of the p-type region into the n-type region, and electrons do the opposite. This creates an electrical imbalance that eventually stops the electrons from moving. Applying a voltage one way makes the imbalance worse, so no current flows. A small voltage the other way overcomes the imbalance and allows current through. The large diode here (both diodes are shown actual size) is used for big power supplies. It will withstand 400 volts in the wrong direction and handle a current of 240 amps.

Tiny diode

Cooling fin

Nut maintains pressure between plates

Oxidized copper plate

Connecting tag

METAL RECTIFIER

Semiconductors were in use throughout much of the thermionic valve era (pp. 28-29). Copper in contact with copper oxide, a semiconductor, conducts electricity much better in one direction than the other – it forms a diode. Stacks of oxidized copper plates were used to "rectify" the alternating voltage of household electricity, creating the steady voltage needed by valves. The cat's whisker detector used in crystal sets also depended on a contact between metal and semiconductor to form a rectifying diode.

Anode stud

Large diode

CARBORUNDUM

When chemically combined with its close relation carbon, silicon forms a hard, often iridescent, semiconducting material called silicon carbide, or carborundum. It was widely used in early radio detectors, but is now employed only as an abrasive.

Development of the transistor

IN 1947 INCREASED UNDERSTANDING of the physics of solids led to the creation of the transistor, a semiconductor amplifier that was to have an impact out of all proportion to its size. The earliest semiconductor devices were diodes (p. 37) which, with their one-way conduction, are still useful for turning alternating into direct current (pp. 22-23). But the transistor could replace a key electronic component, the triode (p. 37), duplicating its ability to amplify and switch without needing its large, fragile glass envelope or power-hungry heater. The transistor was originally conceived as a possible replacement for electromechanical switches in telephone exchanges. Forty years of development have changed it into a microscopic pattern etched into the surface of a slice of silicon (pp. 52-53). Many devices we now take for granted would be unrecognizable without the transistor. A video recorder would need at least eight times the space and a personal computer would fill a room. Both would be unaffordable.

THE MAN IN THE STREET
The transistor lit the fuse to an information explosion which continues today. By the late 1950s this man, who was probably born before electronics, had instant access to news, even standing in the street. Today personal radios and cassette machines are seen in public places everywhere.

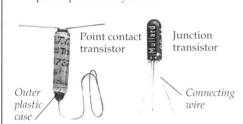

Point contact transistor

Junction transistor

Outer plastic case

Connecting wire

DIFFERENT TYPES OF TRANSISTOR
The transistor has evolved into many different types adapted to different jobs. Those shown here are actual size. Some are good at amplifying small radio frequency signals. Others are slower but can handle large currents and voltages. There are also devices related to the transistor but behaving quite differently. The thyristor, once triggered into conducting electricity, stays switched on without further input, just like a mechanical switch.

Thyristor used in lamp dimmers

BTY79

8C109

Transistor for high-frequency analogue circuits

8736 TIPL770

Power transistor in plastic pack

EARLY TRANSISTORS
William Shockley (1910-1989), leader of the team that invented the point contact transistor, went on to invent the more reliable junction type. Point contact transistors, based directly on the original invention of 1947, were produced commercially until the early 1950s. Two contact wires and a base connection were positioned on a germanium crystal, which was then sealed into a can. These devices were highly unreliable and added a lot of noise to signals. In the junction transistor, the wire probes are replaced by blobs of p-type germanium fused to an n-type base (p.37). These components were the first practical commercial transistors, and were used from about 1950 to 1955.

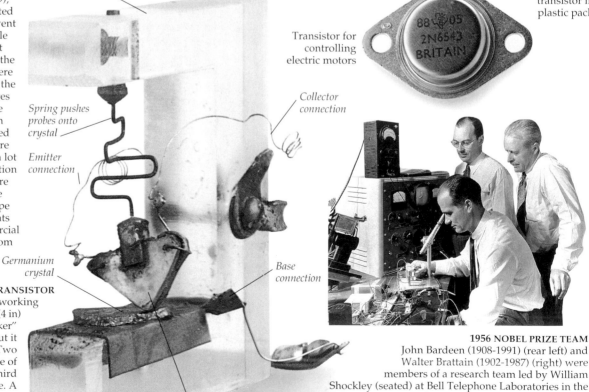

Supporting frame

Spring pushes probes onto crystal

Emitter connection

Germanium crystal

Block holding two wire probes

Transistor for controlling electric motors

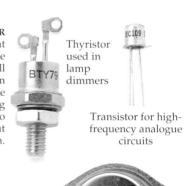

88 05
2N6543
BRITAIN

Collector connection

Base connection

THE FIRST TRANSISTOR
This replica of the first working transistor, which is about 10 cm (4 in) high, resembles the "cat's whisker" detector of early radio sets, but it is a semiconductor amplifier. Two pointed wires probe the surface of a germanium crystal, while a third connection is made to the base. A change in current through one probe causes a larger change in current through the other.

1956 NOBEL PRIZE TEAM
John Bardeen (1908-1991) (rear left) and Walter Brattain (1902-1987) (right) were members of a research team led by William Shockley (seated) at Bell Telephone Laboratories in the USA. In 1947 they demonstrated the first semiconductor amplifier. Their work was the result of Bell's deliberate policy of searching for new technologies that could improve the telephone system.

HOW A FIELD EFFECT TRANSISTOR WORKS

A field effect transistor (FET) was patented in 1935 by German physicist Oskar Heil (born 1908), but did not work. Computer chips are composed almost entirely of FETs. Two n-type regions ("source" and "drain") are separated by a p-type "channel". This has too few electrons to pass current, but if an insulated electrode (the "gate") is made positive, the sparse electrons of the p-type material crowd into the channel, turning the transistor on. Other kinds of FET are made with n-type channels, or using a p-n junction instead of an insulated gate, or reducing rather than increasing the number of current carriers in the channel.

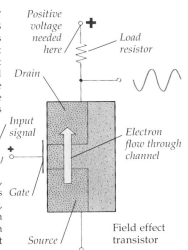

Positive voltage needed here

Load resistor

Drain

Input signal

Electron flow through channel

Gate

Source

Field effect transistor

TRANSISTOR PORTABLE RADIO

To most people in the 1960s, "transistor" meant a little portable radio, rather than the revolutionary device inside. It was more the low power consumption than the small size of the transistor that made it possible to carry it around. Small portables had already been made using valves, but their batteries were either too heavy or ran out quickly.

Tuning control

Volume control

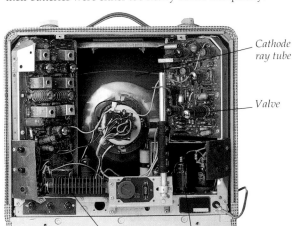

Cathode ray tube

Valve

1960s black-and-white television

Metal rectifier

Valve

HOW A BIPOLAR TRANSISTOR WORKS

The bipolar transistor is widely used in amplifiers. It has a p-type layer (the "base") sandwiched between two n-type layers (the "emitter" and "collector"). It is like two diodes (p. 37) connected back to back, so current cannot normally flow. Making the base more positive than the emitter allows electrons from the emitter to get into the base. Once there, most of them get to the collector. So electrons travel from emitter to collector, controlled by the base voltage. Holes, too, carry some current – hence the name "bipolar". This is an "npn" transistor. There are also "pnp" transistors, with an n-type base between p-type emitter and collector.

Positive voltage needed here

Output signal

Load resistor

Collector

A few electrons are lost

Electrons move in this direction

Emitter

Base

Bipolar transistor

TRANSISTORIZED TELEVISION

Early television sets (above) used only valves. By the 1970s valves had been replaced by transistors. The resulting chassis (right) is dominated by the tube that displays the picture (pp. 44-45) and the components that supply the high voltages it needs. The transistors themselves are almost invisible. By the 1980s most transistors had become even smaller, disappearing inside integrated circuits (pp. 52-53).

Cathode ray tube

High-voltage connector

High-voltage generator

Tuning control circuit

Picture circuit

Pre-set resistor

Loudspeaker

Aerial connector

1970s colour television set with transistors

Transistor

Power supply circuit

Scanning circuit

High frequencies

WHEN ELECTROMAGNETIC WAVES ENCOUNTER a circuit that is not much smaller than they are, strange things can happen. As the frequency rises into the "microwave" region above a billion hertz (the unit of frequency), the wavelength gets close to the size of a circuit board, and the simple idea of a circuit begins to fade away. Conductors start to span parts of the wave that are out of step with each other, so that voltages and currents no longer add up as expected. Passive components misbehave, with resistors turning into inductors, and inductors into capacitors. Active components can stop working altogether. Electronics at these frequencies is almost a different subject. Components and circuits have to be made smaller, or the way waves travel allowed for, or both. Even electrons can be too sluggish for microwaves, so special semiconductors are often needed in microwave amplifiers. But there are good reasons for taming these exotic waves. Microwaves can carry more information. They keep to straight paths, which is useful for linking cities. Unlike longer waves, they can penetrate the Earth's outer atmosphere to allow communication with space.

THE MICROWAVE OVEN
When high-power microwaves became available in the 1940s workers noticed that they could make things hot. It was American engineer Percy Le Baron Spencer (1894-1970) who in 1945 found a microwave-melted sweet in his pocket and conceived the idea of the microwave oven.

Large objects cast shadows

Runway

Aeroplane

AIRPORT RADAR IMAGE
This is London's Heathrow Airport as seen by a radar at its centre. As the frequency of radio waves rises, their wavelength falls and they begin to behave more like light. With a wavelength of only millimetres, this radar can pick out details of aircraft and buildings. The beam spreads at the edges, making the picture there less clear.

Echo comes back

Radio pulses sent out

Echoes from near objects appear near centre

Radar antenna rotates

Display

Electron beam scans from centre to edge

HOW RADAR WORKS
The rotating antenna of a radar alternately sends out short pulses of radio waves and listens for their echoes. After each pulse, a spot on the display sweeps from the centre to the edge at an angle matching that of the antenna. Echoes from near objects come back sooner, so appear nearer the centre of the display.

Large object casts shadow

Returning echoes sent to display

RANDALL AND BOOT MAGNETRON
Clear radar images of distant objects demand a high-power source of microwaves. British physicists John Randall (1905-1984) and Harry Boot (1917-1983) of Birmingham University in England put this prototype magnetron together in 1940, using bits and pieces from their laboratory. The magnetron whirled electrons around in the field of a powerful electromagnet (p. 18) to generate waves 10 cm (4 in) long with a power of 40 watts. This is the ancestor of the magnetron that is used to power every microwave oven.

Sealing wax

Coin to plug up hole

Water-cooling tube

Copper anode block inside

Connection to vacuum pump

Plate against which one pole of electromagnet fits

Water-cooling tube

1946-107

WAAF PLOTTING AIRCRAFT
Radar is a way of detecting objects and measuring their position by firing bursts of high-frequency radio waves at them and timing the echoes that come back. It was developed from the 1930s onwards. This member of the Women's Auxiliary Air Force (WAAF) is plotting targets by radar during the Second World War (1939-1945).

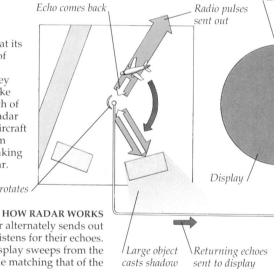

SATELLITE TELEVISION

The idea of broadcasting from a satellite that appears to stand still in the sky is not new. But only recently has microwave technology become cheap and reliable enough to allow an affordable service. Microwaves at frequencies of over 10 billion hertz are used, which easily penetrate the atmosphere. The domestic satellite television dish is a miniature version of the huge dishes used to beam signals up to satellites (p. 13). The amount of power in the incoming television signal, after its 70,000 km (44,000 mile) journey through space, is unbelievably tiny. But the low-noise block still manages to amplify it and also shift its frequency down to something more easily handled by the satellite receiver inside the house.

Perforations in reflector to make it less conspicuous

Low-noise block amplifies signal and reduces its frequency

Horn with weather shield

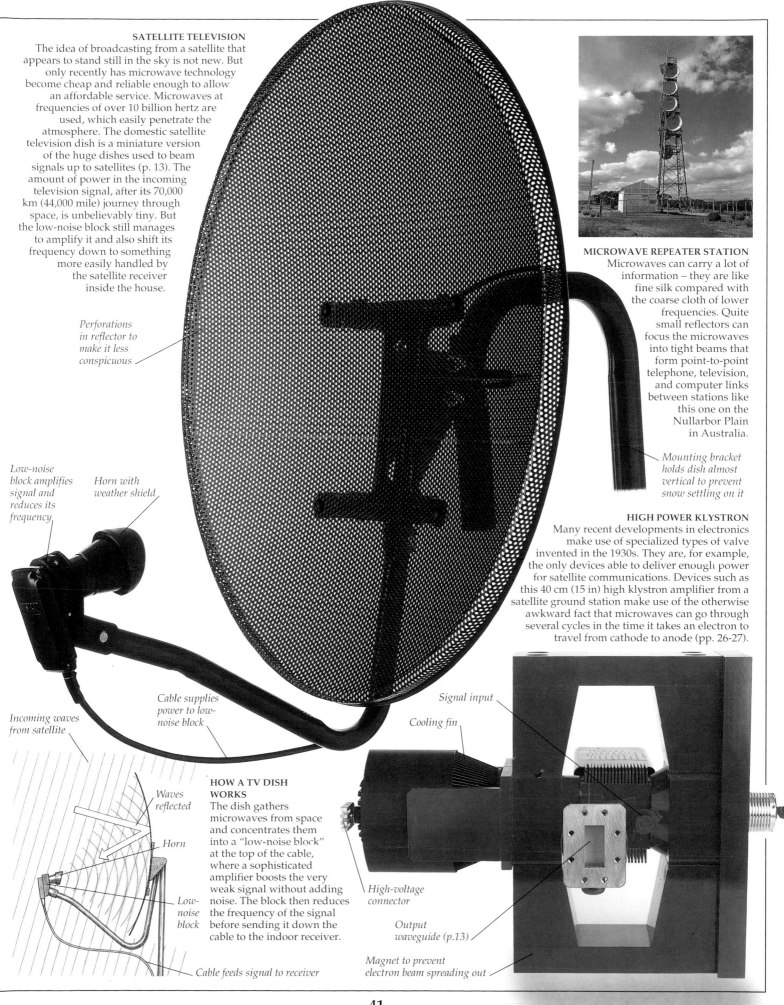

MICROWAVE REPEATER STATION

Microwaves can carry a lot of information – they are like fine silk compared with the coarse cloth of lower frequencies. Quite small reflectors can focus the microwaves into tight beams that form point-to-point telephone, television, and computer links between stations like this one on the Nullarbor Plain in Australia.

Mounting bracket holds dish almost vertical to prevent snow settling on it

HIGH POWER KLYSTRON

Many recent developments in electronics make use of specialized types of valve invented in the 1930s. They are, for example, the only devices able to deliver enough power for satellite communications. Devices such as this 40 cm (15 in) high klystron amplifier from a satellite ground station make use of the otherwise awkward fact that microwaves can go through several cycles in the time it takes an electron to travel from cathode to anode (pp. 26-27).

Incoming waves from satellite

Cable supplies power to low-noise block

Signal input

Cooling fin

HOW A TV DISH WORKS

The dish gathers microwaves from space and concentrates them into a "low-noise block" at the top of the cable, where a sophisticated amplifier boosts the very weak signal without adding noise. The block then reduces the frequency of the signal before sending it down the cable to the indoor receiver.

Waves reflected

Horn

Low-noise block

High-voltage connector

Output waveguide (p.13)

Cable feeds signal to receiver

Magnet to prevent electron beam spreading out

41

Translating useful signals

IF ELECTRONICS PRODUCED ONLY ELECTRICAL EFFECTS, it would be of limited value. To do useful things, it needs devices that can translate voltages and currents into the sounds, lights, and forces of everyday life. Likewise, electronic devices need the physical world to be translated into electrical signals. Devices that can perform these translations are called transducers. They are able to change the type of energy that is carrying information without changing the information itself. A familiar example is the loudspeaker, which converts electric power into sound. But transducers can now detect everything from radioactivity to smoke and produce effects ranging from ear-splitting sound to gently changing light. To do this, they use a wide range of processes including electromagnetism, the effect of light on semiconductors, and the variation of resistance with stress and temperature.

DAVID HUGHES (1831-1900)
Hughes was born in London but emigrated to America, where he became a professor of music and invented a successful telegraph. Back in London, experimenting with sound, he discovered an effective transducer. It was so sensitive that he thought of it as a sort of "sound microscope", and called it the "microphone".

Wooden base helps pick up sound

Connecting wires

Loose nail vibrates with sound

Nails stuck with wax

THREE NAILS DETECTING SOUND
Hughes discovered that loose electrical contacts are extraordinarily sensitive to vibrations, including sound. This 1878 arrangement of three ordinary nails must rate as one of the world's simplest scientific breakthroughs. Microphones using Hughes's principle are more efficient transducers than Bell's telephone (below). This one was so responsive that, even without electronic amplification, it could detect a fly's footstep. Connected to a modern tape recorder, it will produce an acceptable recording.

THE RADIO MICROPHONE
Perhaps the most famous transducer of them all, this microphone was used by the BBC from 1934 until 1959. Tiny pressure changes caused by sound waves make the aluminium ribbon, less than a thousandth of a millimetre thick, vibrate between the poles of a large magnet, generating currents that mimic the sound wave with remarkable accuracy.

Wooden case

Currents in wire make diaphragm vibrate

Magnet

Iron diaphragm

EARLY TELEPHONE
The first practical transducer that could deal with a continuously changing signal was Alexander Graham Bell's telephone of 1876. It could convert sound into electromagnetic waves (pp. 12-13) and back again. Vibrations of a thin iron diaphragm set up currents in wires wound around a magnet. Alternatively, currents in the wires could make the diaphragm vibrate. Putting instruments like this at each end of a long wire, Bell made the first effective telephone.

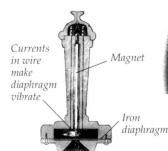

A WORLD SERVICE
The electronic chain that carries the voice of the BBC around the world begins and ends with transducers – a microphone in a studio and a loudspeaker in a distant listener's home. This microphone was developed from the AXBT unit (right).

BBC-Marconi AXBT ribbon microphone with cover

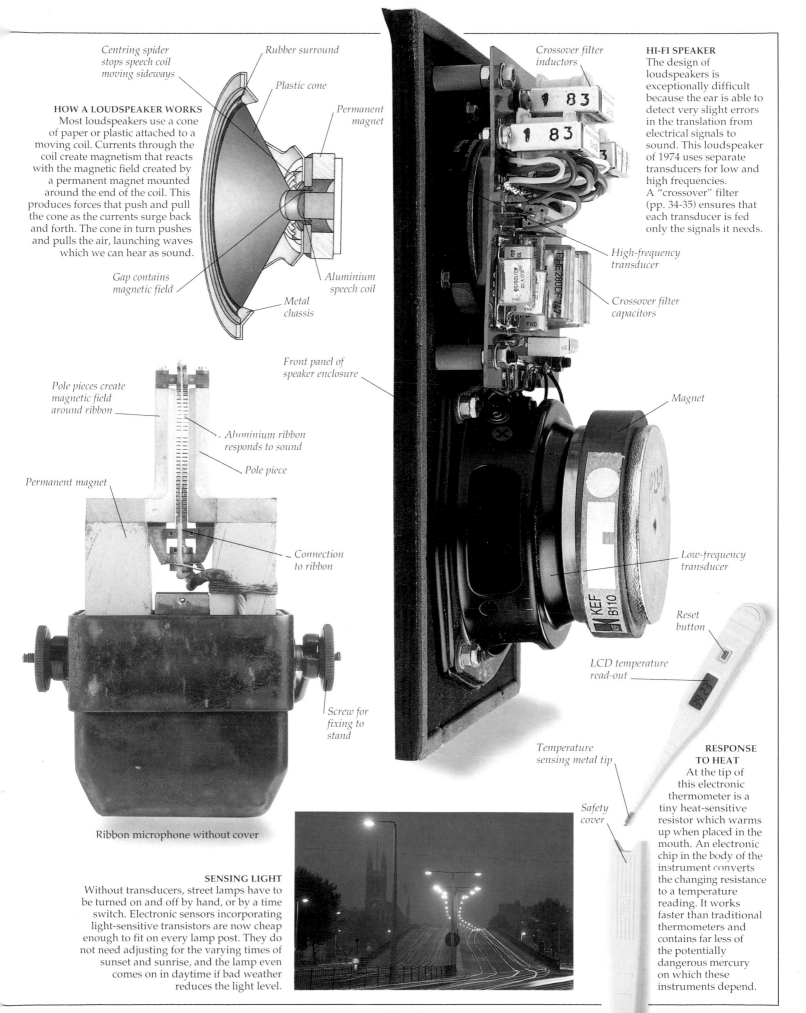

HOW A LOUDSPEAKER WORKS

Most loudspeakers use a cone of paper or plastic attached to a moving coil. Currents through the coil create magnetism that reacts with the magnetic field created by a permanent magnet mounted around the end of the coil. This produces forces that push and pull the cone as the currents surge back and forth. The cone in turn pushes and pulls the air, launching waves which we can hear as sound.

Centring spider stops speech coil moving sideways

Rubber surround

Plastic cone

Permanent magnet

Gap contains magnetic field

Aluminium speech coil

Metal chassis

Crossover filter inductors

HI-FI SPEAKER

The design of loudspeakers is exceptionally difficult because the ear is able to detect very slight errors in the translation from electrical signals to sound. This loudspeaker of 1974 uses separate transducers for low and high frequencies. A "crossover" filter (pp. 34-35) ensures that each transducer is fed only the signals it needs.

High-frequency transducer

Crossover filter capacitors

Front panel of speaker enclosure

Magnet

Low-frequency transducer

Pole pieces create magnetic field around ribbon

Aluminium ribbon responds to sound

Pole piece

Permanent magnet

Connection to ribbon

Screw for fixing to stand

Ribbon microphone without cover

Reset button

LCD temperature read-out

Temperature sensing metal tip

Safety cover

RESPONSE TO HEAT

At the tip of this electronic thermometer is a tiny heat-sensitive resistor which warms up when placed in the mouth. An electronic chip in the body of the instrument converts the changing resistance to a temperature reading. It works faster than traditional thermometers and contains far less of the potentially dangerous mercury on which these instruments depend.

SENSING LIGHT

Without transducers, street lamps have to be turned on and off by hand, or by a time switch. Electronic sensors incorporating light-sensitive transistors are now cheap enough to fit on every lamp post. They do not need adjusting for the varying times of sunset and sunrise, and the lamp even comes on in daytime if bad weather reduces the light level.

The visual connection

Looking at a piece of electronic equipment, the first thing most people notice is the display. This is no accident. Displays are there to attract attention, to communicate. Although progress has been made with electronic speech, most interaction with electronic systems is visual. Their displays range from a computer screen to a simple lamp that warns you something is switched on. Although computer graphics can look impressively modern, they are usually seen on a device that started life in 1897 – the cathode ray tube (CRT). In spite of efforts to find a slimmer, cheaper alternative, the CRT still shows the best pictures. It offers more detail, higher brightness, and can be viewed over a wider angle than any of its competitors. But if you do not need pictures, there are plenty of alternatives. Liquid crystal displays (LCDs) use almost no power. Light-emitting diodes (LEDs) or electromechanical displays can make large, clear signs. Vacuum fluorescent displays use the same principle as the CRT to produce the glowing green numbers seen on video recorders.

LARGER THAN LIFE
The screens of cathode ray tubes (CRTs) cannot be made very big, although small CRTs when used with lenses can project images 2 m (6 ft 6 in) wide, and projectors using an arc lamp controlled by a CRT can do even better. But discharge tubes like the ones used in advertising signs can form a huge screen. Electronics sends a different bit of the picture to each of the thousands of red, green and blue tubes. This type of display has become a regular feature of international sporting events, giving each spectator a close-up view. Here runners are seen lining up for the start of the marathon at the Los Angeles Olympics of 1984.

Connection for high voltage to accelerate electrons toward screen

COLOUR TELEVISION TUBE
This tube is really three cathode ray tubes in one, showing pictures in red, green, and blue. Together these three colours can match almost any colour. The tube has three electron guns in the neck and a metal shadow mask near the screen, positioned so that any point on the screen receives electrons from only one gun. All the points that receive electrons from the "red" gun are coated with a chemical phosphor which glows red when electrons hit it, and likewise for green and blue. The result is a full-colour picture made from stripes of just three colours.

Connecting pin for picture signals

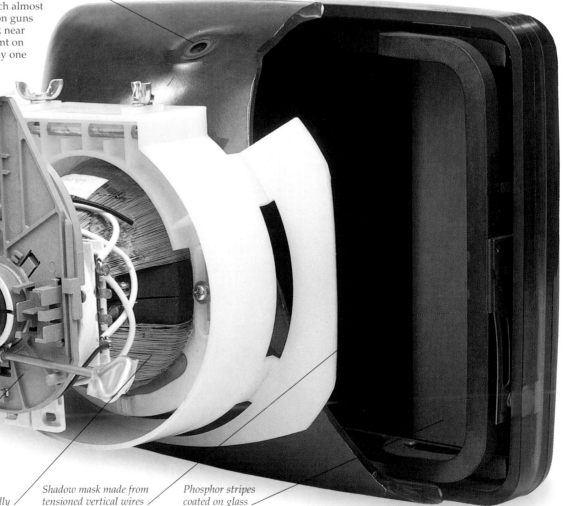

Three electron guns hidden inside shared anode

Movable magnet adjusts colour purity and lines up three pictures

Scanning coil sweeps electron beams across screen magnetically

Shadow mask made from tensioned vertical wires

Phosphor stripes coated on glass

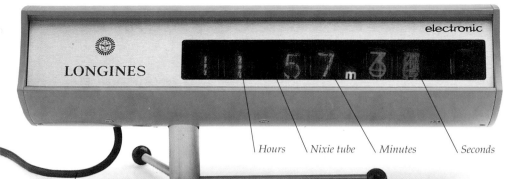

LONGINES CLOCK
Digital displays were a rarity in the early 1960s when this clock was made. The numbers are produced by "Nixie" tubes based on neon lamps of the sort still used to indicate when electrical appliances are switched on. Control logic (pp. 50-51), connected to electrodes inside, makes the orange discharge form around one of ten display electrodes shaped to show the digits 0-9.

Hours   *Nixie tube*   *Minutes*   *Seconds*

Mains lead

AMSTERDAM AIRPORT
Electromechanical devices, like this one at Amsterdam's international airport in the Netherlands, make large, clear displays. They have the advantage of using power only when the message is actually changing. At other times the mechanism retains the last message sent.

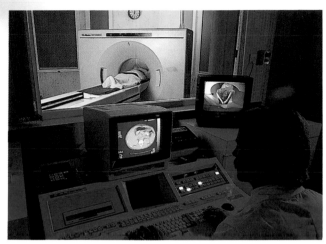

BODY SCANNING
Computer technology for business, science, and medicine depends on displays to link people with machines. A powerful computer in this scanner combines many X-ray measurements to form a detailed picture of the patient's body, but without the colour display that reveals the picture to the radiographer its work would be much less useful.

Transparent electrode

Light

Top polarizer

Polarization of light twisted through right angle by liquid crystal

No voltage applied

Liquid crystal molecules

Bottom polarizer

Glass plate

LCD display OFF

Mirror

HOW LCD WORKS
Liquid crystals are liquids with a regular structure. Some can polarize light, like sunglasses. Trapped between glass plates with special surfaces, their molecules lie flat and form a twisted path that guides light through a pair of crossed polarizers. But a voltage between the plates makes the molecules stand on end, they can no longer guide the light, and the display turns dark.

Coated surface makes molecules line up with direction of polarizer

Voltage applied

No polarizing effect so light blocked

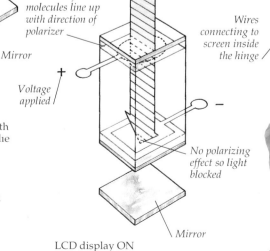

Mirror

LCD display ON

LCD screen illuminated from behind

PORTABLE DISPLAY
Liquid crystal displays have no rivals for portable equipment because they consume almost no power. More advanced displays incorporate transistors within the screen itself to look after each of the thousands of picture elements, simplifying the circuits needed to control them. By making each point of the screen a cluster of red, green, and blue elements, full colour pictures can be displayed.

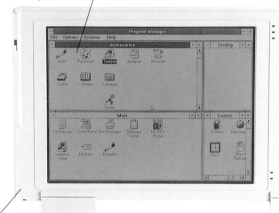

Lid folds down for carrying

Wires connecting to screen inside the hinge

Keyboard

Analogue and digital

ELECTRONIC SYSTEMS CAN HANDLE INFORMATION in one of two forms. Signals may vary smoothly and continuously, like the rapid variations of air pressure we hear as sound, or they may consist of only a limited number of symbols, like the letters of a message. Analogue electronics translates smoothly varying quantities into smoothly varying signals, while digital systems deal with definite symbols. Although digital systems obey the fundamental principles of analogue electronics, their inputs and outputs can only switch between a few – usually two – values, which are strung together to form codes. This obviously suits things like letters or numbers. It is not so obvious that digital electronics can also handle analogue signals, but many smoothly varying quantities can in fact be reduced to numbers and then treated like any other numerical data. This brings advantages. Digital signals can be manipulated by computers, and are also less affected by interference.

INTRODUCING BINARY
German philosopher and mathematician Gottfried Leibniz (1646-1716) brought the significance of the binary system to the attention of other mathematicians in 1703. He was mainly interested in it as a proof that the world was created by God. The system is a way of writing numbers using only two symbols. Because electronic switches flip between just two states, it is the best way of representing numbers in digital electronic equipment.

HOW BINARY WORKS
Traditional kitchen scales use weights of 8, 4, 2, and 1 units. The weights making up a given quantity can be recorded using a "1" to show a weight is needed and a "0" to show it is not. The weights making up 14 units would be written "1110", meaning "use 8, 4, and 2 but not 1". The binary system works in just this way. Binary digits – "bits" – show which fixed numbers must be added to make a given number. The last bit on the right shows whether or not 1 is needed. Bits to the left of this indicate the need for 2, 4, and so on. The number 25 becomes "11001", with the bits standing for 16, 8, and 1 set to "1" because these numbers add up to 25. Since 4 and 2 are not needed, their bits are set to "0".

Adding flour until the scales balance gives the required quantity

SAMPLING THE ACTION
Moving pictures are an illusion built up from still pictures. Rapid action can reveal this, as when wagon wheels appear to roll backwards in the movies. Digital sampling also works by taking "snapshots". An analogue signal (top) is measured or "sampled" at regular intervals and the measurements expressed in binary code to form a digital signal (centre). The conversion is never exact and, if the sampling is done too slowly (below), the decoded signal may be completely misleading, as with the wagon wheels.

Sample value

Digital signal

Sample value

Misleading signal

Weights representing desired quantity placed on scale first

2 unit weight

4 unit weight

8 unit weight

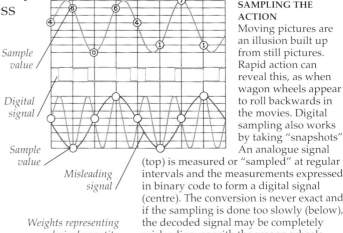

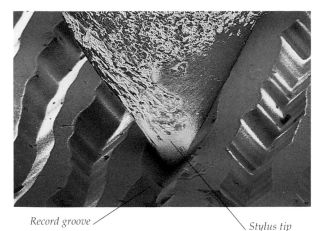

Record groove — *Stylus tip*

NOISY SURFACE

Analogue recording reigned supreme in the home until the 1980s. Long-playing records (LPs), moulded in vinyl plastic, appeared in the late 1940s. They were a direct development from earlier records, which had coarser grooves and higher playing speed. This scanning electron micrograph of modern record grooves shows how they capture every nuance of the original sound wave. But because the shape of the wave is translated directly into the shape of the surface, any damage must appear as noise – usually a loud thump as the stylus runs over a scratch. This inability to distinguish between signal and noise is a basic limitation of analogue systems.

ALEC REEVES (1902-1971)

The idea of converting speech to digital code came to British telephone engineer Alec Reeves as early as 1937. He was working on systems that could send many telephone calls down one cable to link exchanges in two different cities. He showed that sampling and analogue-to-digital conversion could reduce telephone calls to a stream of on-off pulses. Unlike analogue signals, these pulses would hardly be affected by interference from other channels sharing the same cable. This would allow a cable to carry more calls without annoying "cross-talk". His "pulse code modulation" technique had to wait until the 1970s for electronic devices advanced enough to make it practical. It is now used for long-distance links everywhere.

CONVERTING SIGNALS

A modern telephone exchange is really a specialized computer. It is able to treat calls as if they were computer data because every call passes through an analogue-to-digital converter before the exchange sends it on its way. A digital link speeds it to the destination exchange, where a digital-to-analogue converter recreates the original signal before passing it to the telephone being called.

BETTER SOUND QUALITY

A compact disc is smaller than an LP, plays for over twice as long with better sound, and is unaffected by minor damage. All this is possible because the sound is converted into a string of digital codes, which appear on the disc as microscopic pits that can be read by a laser beam. A complicated coding system ensures that there is usually enough data elsewhere on the disc to fill in any parts of the recording made unreadable by scratches.

CONVERTING QUANTITIES

A fish can be any weight. Its weight is an analogue quantity. Matching it with weights whose total can only change in fixed steps is an analogue-to-digital conversion. Weighing flour (left) is a digital-to-analogue conversion, because the fixed weights are balanced by a continuously variable weight of flour.

Fish placed on scale first

Weights added to balance fish, thus representing its weight as a definite number

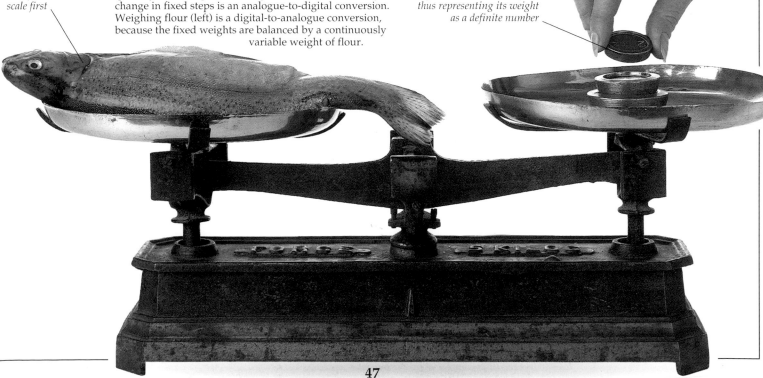

Signals and codes

PEOPLE EVERYWHERE MAKE SIMILAR SOUNDS when they talk, but this does not mean they can all understand each other. They can communicate only if they share a code that links sounds to meanings – a language. In the same way, electronic systems all use similar voltages, currents, and waves, but successful communication between them demands that they use an agreed code. Most television sets will only work with signals conforming to a particular national standard. In another country, where television is coded differently, they will not produce recognizable pictures. Unlike human languages, electronic codes vary widely in efficiency. Some earlier codes are inefficient, using a wider range of transmitted frequencies (pp. 14-15) than is really necessary. This is because efficient coding often demands computing power that has only really been available since the advent of the microprocessor (pp. 56-57).

GETTING THE MESSAGE
People also need a common code if they are to communicate. The referee's whistle is not always enough. The card system offers a clearly agreed code. When a player sees the yellow card he gets the message "you have been warned", whatever his native language.

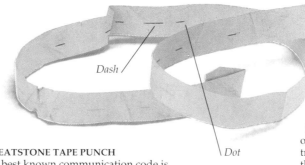

Dash

Dot

MORSE TAPE
Early communication systems needed skilled operators to interpret the language of primitive machines. This tape was produced by a Morse inker that simply marked the received dots and dashes on a strip of paper. A trained clerk was needed to translate the code into ordinary writing that the customers could read.

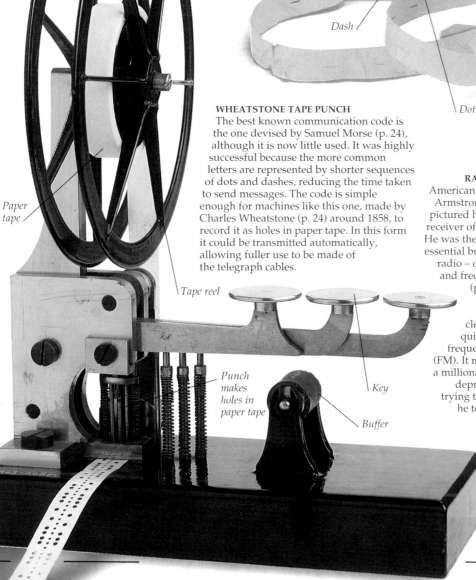

WHEATSTONE TAPE PUNCH
The best known communication code is the one devised by Samuel Morse (p. 24), although it is now little used. It was highly successful because the more common letters are represented by shorter sequences of dots and dashes, reducing the time taken to send messages. The code is simple enough for machines like this one, made by Charles Wheatstone (p. 24) around 1858, to record it as holes in paper tape. In this form it could be transmitted automatically, allowing fuller use to be made of the telegraph cables.

Paper tape

Tape reel

Punch makes holes in paper tape

Key

Buffer

RADIO INVENTOR
American engineer Edwin Armstrong (1890-1954) is pictured here with a radio receiver of his own design. He was the inventor of two essential building blocks of radio – oscillators (p. 33) and frequency changers (p. 35). In 1933 he also invented a system offering clear sound with a quiet background – frequency modulation (FM). It made Armstrong a millionaire, but in 1954, depressed by people trying to steal his ideas, he took his own life.

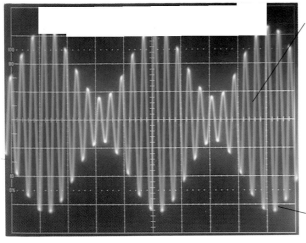

Carrier wave

Tips of wave give shape of sound wave

COMMUNICATION THEORY

In 1948 the American engineer Claude Shannon (b. 1916) revealed a way of measuring information in communications systems. It was based on the idea that the more unexpected a signal is, the more information it conveys. He also developed a way of calculating the maximum rate at which information can be sent through a given channel. His work sets out the fundamental rules within which communications engineers must operate. It also allows them to see how efficient a code is by checking its rate of transmission against the theoretical limit.

AMPLITUDE MODULATION

A radio wave can be received from far away, but in itself says only that the transmitter is switched on. To convey useful information, the steady "carrier" wave must be "modulated" in some way. Amplitude modulation (AM), displayed here on an oscilloscope, transmits the shape of a sound wave as a variation in the strength of the carrier wave.

Spectrum contains many frequencies

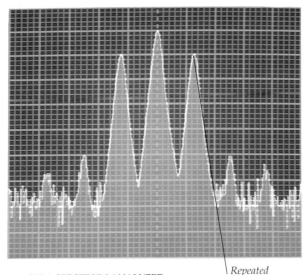

No signal here

Some frequencies have low power

FREQUENCY MODULATION

Frequency modulation (FM) is another way of varying a carrier wave to convey information. The shape of a sound wave is transmitted by varying the frequency, rather than the strength of the wave. The modulated carrier has a complex spectrum occupying a wide range of frequencies, but it makes up for this by being highly resistant to interference.

AM ON A SPECTRUM ANALYZER

All radio transmissions contain many frequencies (pp. 14-15). Other stations have to avoid these frequencies if there is not to be interference. Amplitude modulation is inefficient because, as this spectrum analyzer picture shows, both halves of its spectrum are exactly the same shape (although one is reversed), wasting frequencies that other stations could use.

Repeated information

READING A BAR CODE

The stripes of a bar code represent a number that identifies a particular product and pack. The code is standardized so that machines all over the world can read it. In the most widely used type, each digit is represented by stripes totalling 7 units wide. The thinnest lines and spaces are 1 unit wide, and the thicker ones up to 4 units wide. The digit codes are not based on the simple binary system (pp. 46-47), and the code for a particular digit varies with its position in the number. This helps prevent errors.

Thinnest line reads as "1"

780863 185779

Each digit code is 7 units wide

Thinnest space reads as "0"

BAR CODE READER

Bar code readers can be fixed or hand-held. Fixed readers normally use a laser to scan the code, but hand-held models sometimes incorporate a device rather like a tiny television camera. In either case the result is a string of on/off pulses which can be decoded by a computer. A "bleep" signals successful decoding. The long stripes allow the code to be read at an angle (multiple laser beams also help with this), while clever coding helps the machine to detect errors and read the code upside down.

Bar code

Light from reader

Logical rules

GEORGE BOOLE (1815-1864)
British mathematician George Boole was entirely self taught. He never took a degree, yet became a professor of mathematics and in 1854 published his algebra, a way of combining symbols that perfectly expresses the rules of logic. Using this, complicated rules can be written clearly and often simplified.

Eᴀʀʟʏ ᴄᴏᴍᴘᴜᴛᴇʀs ᴡᴇʀᴇ sometimes called "electronic brains" because they amazed people by being able to work out logical problems. In fact, computers are nothing like human brains, which can easily solve problems that defeat computers, but are often confused by logical puzzles. Boolean algebra enables us to take such problems one step at a time and reach the right conclusion. This is just what computers do, but millions of times faster than humans can. Engineers give computers this power by building the rules of logic into electronic circuits called "gates", which are switches that turn on or off when presented with the right combination of inputs. Digital circuits formed by connecting gates together can be made to obey any desired rule, as long as it is completely clear.

VENN DIAGRAM
The basic Boolean operations are ᴀɴᴅ, ᴏʀ and ɴᴏᴛ. Pictures like this, based on the type of diagram invented around 1880 by the British logician John Venn (1834-1923), can be used to illustrate these operations. Out of many possible shapes and colours, one circle contains only cubes (of several colours), while the other contains only red bricks (of several shapes). Where the circles overlap, the bricks must be red ᴀɴᴅ cubes. The two circles together contain bricks that are red ᴏʀ cubes. In the area outside the circles, the bricks are ɴᴏᴛ red ᴀɴᴅ ɴᴏᴛ cubes.

Circle contains red bricks of different shapes

THE LANGUAGE OF LOGIC

The basic Boolean operations are ᴀɴᴅ ($\cap$), ᴏʀ ($\cup$) and ɴᴏᴛ ($\overline{}$). These and others can be carried out electronically by logic gates. Each gate has a special symbol used in drawing the diagrams which show how the gates are to be connected together. Some gates are shown below together with Boolean equations giving the rules they follow.

$\begin{matrix}A\\B\end{matrix}$ —⊐D— C	AND gate:	$C = A \cap B$
$\begin{matrix}A\\B\end{matrix}$ —⊐D— C	OR gate:	$C = A \cup B$
A —▷o— C	Inverter:	$C = \overline{A}$
$\begin{matrix}A\\B\end{matrix}$ —⊐Do— C	NAND gate:	$C = \overline{A \cap B}$
$\begin{matrix}A\\B\end{matrix}$ —⊐Do— C	NOR gate:	$C = \overline{A \cup B}$

Boolean algebra can be used to write down rules, which will be obeyed by logic gates connected together to give the same Boolean expression. A car seat belt warning device might obey the rule "if there is weight on the seat and the belt is not fastened, flash the warning lamp", or more simply "lamp = weight ᴀɴᴅ ɴᴏᴛ fastened". Boolean algebra allows the corresponding statement $L = W \cap \overline{F}$ to be changed to $\overline{L} = \overline{W} \cup F$, which says that the lamp should stay off if there is no weight or the belt is fastened.

The seat belt circuit would look like this:

or, using a different set of gates, like this:

TWEEDLEDUM AND TWEEDLEDEE

Lewis Carroll (1832-1898), best known for his *Alice* books, was also a first-rate mathematician with a special interest in logic. His books abound with sly references to the more absurd aspects of the subject. Tweedledum and Tweedledee escape their everlasting argument only when something strictly illogical – a gigantic crow – comes along.

CONVERTING CODES

Logic circuits are well suited to carrying out code conversions. This shows part of a circuit that converts the digits 0-9 represented in the binary system into patterns that people can read. The interconnected gates and inverter ensure that the lower right segment of the display stays on for every digit except 2, which is represented by the binary code "0010".

0	0	1	0

"0010" represents 2

0	0	1	1

"0011" represents 3

Inverter

OR gate with one input = "1"

OR gate with both inputs = "0"

Segment output is "0"

Segment output is "1"

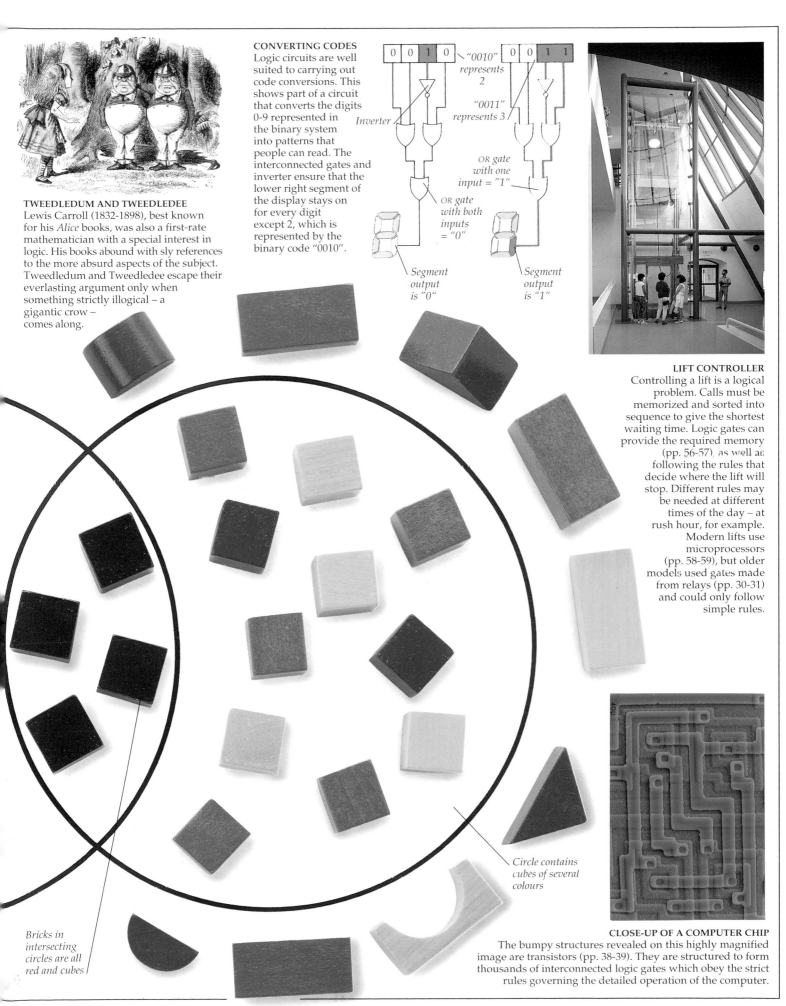

LIFT CONTROLLER

Controlling a lift is a logical problem. Calls must be memorized and sorted into sequence to give the shortest waiting time. Logic gates can provide the required memory (pp. 56-57), as well as following the rules that decide where the lift will stop. Different rules may be needed at different times of the day – at rush hour, for example. Modern lifts use microprocessors (pp. 58-59), but older models used gates made from relays (pp. 30-31) and could only follow simple rules.

Circle contains cubes of several colours

Bricks in intersecting circles are all red and cubes

CLOSE-UP OF A COMPUTER CHIP

The bumpy structures revealed on this highly magnified image are transistors (pp. 38-39). They are structured to form thousands of interconnected logic gates which obey the strict rules governing the detailed operation of the computer.

Glass tube

Tuning
coil

Tuning control

Integrated circuits

UNTIL THE 1960S ELECTRONICS ENGINEERS were limited in what they could do by the size of valves and transistors. Engineers have always sought ways to pack more into less. A first attempt at an integrated circuit was made by Siegmund Loewe in 1926. The first semiconductor integrated circuit was made by Jack Kilby in 1958. It incorporated several transistors on one piece of semiconductor, but there was no way of connecting them together except by hand. The answer was the planar process of 1959, which etches transistors into a silicon surface using photographic techniques (pp. 54-55). The silicon over their active regions is converted into inert oxide or nitride. The resulting transistors are tough and flat, making connection easy. By 1962, with further development of the planar process to connect transistors together with metal tracks, the first truly integrated circuits, commonly known as "chips", were finding their way into electronics.

EARLY INTEGRATED CIRCUIT
German engineer Siegmund Loewe (1885-1962) developed several vacuum tubes which included in one envelope nearly all the components – resistors, capacitors and valves – needed to make a radio. The base of this compact receiver provides only variable capacitors and an interchangeable coil for tuning. Everything else is in the tube.

Recording level meter

Manual rewind handle

Pinch wheel

1950S TAPE RECORDER
The change in scale brought about by integrated circuits is well illustrated by the way the tape recorder has shrunk in size over the years. Improvements in electric motors and the development of compact cassettes have also helped. This professional tape machine was a triumph of miniaturization when it was made in the early 1950s. It substituted some of the first transistors for the valves of previous models. But its amplifiers alone occupy more space than the whole of a personal stereo of 1990. (The two machines are shown here in proportion.)

Tape spool

Loudspeaker

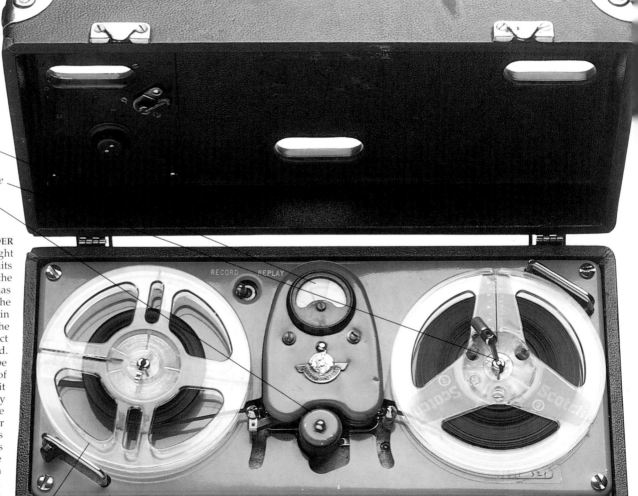

JACK KILBY (B. 1923)

In 1952 Kilby, an American electronics engineer, realized that because transistors were small, the space taken up by their connecting wires was significant. Packing a lot of separate transistors into a small space produced an unworkable maze. In 1958 he demonstrated the first circuit, including resistors, capacitors, and transistors, ever made from a single piece of semiconductor.

Earphone lead doubles as aerial

CARD RADIO

This Japanese pocket radio, made in 1983, has all the electronics needed for an FM receiver integrated into one slim chip, mounted in a case the size of a credit card and not much thicker. The chip itself occupies only a fraction of the space – most of the space is used to accommodate batteries and the large tuning capacitor, which in more recent designs would be replaced by a tiny diode (pp. 36-37).

Light-emitting diode display

Earphone

Tuning control operates variable capacitor

Frequency scale

SINCLAIR CALCULATOR

This pocket calculator was made in Britain by Sinclair, one of the first companies to offer miniaturized electronic equipment. Calculators became widely available in the early 1970s as one of the first fruits of integrated circuit technology. They swept aside traditional calculating aids like the slide rule and abacus (p. 8) that had been used for generations. They squeezed computing power that formerly required a large cabinet into the space of a shirt pocket.

Key pad

Inside the package

Integrated circuits can do jobs ranging from precision amplification to high-speed calculation. But they all look much the same on the outside, and even breaking the package open reveals little. With working parts as small as a thousandth of a millimetre across, the features which distinguish one from another can be seen only under a powerful microscope.

Battery compartment

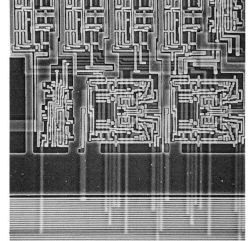

MAGNIFIED CHIP

Only through a powerful microscope is it possible to get some idea of the intricacies etched on the surface of the integrated circuit.

Plastic package

Pins

Volume control

Recording level display

Cassette

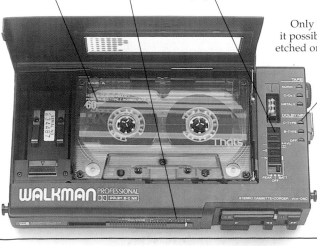

Noise reduction

1990S PERSONAL STEREO

With the arrival of the truly personal stereo, listening on the move has become a major craze. This professional machine depends on integrated circuits to cram advanced facilities such as stereo recording, noise reduction, and provision for different kinds of tape into a pocket-sized package.

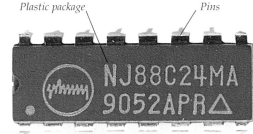

PACKAGED INTEGRATED CHIP

The problem of interconnection still exists even when many transistors have been integrated into one chip. In this simple integrated circuit, the actual slice of silicon inside (right) is dwarfed by the packaging needed to accommodate the connections to the pins that plug into a printed circuit board (pp. 22-23).

Silicon chip

Making microchips

MICROCHIPS ARE AMONG THE MOST INTRICATE DEVICES ever made. Although the largest integrated circuit is only the size of a thumbnail, a drawing showing everything on it would be bigger than a detailed map of a major city. This level of complexity allows integrated circuits to do jobs that once required rooms full of equipment. Designing and making such devices is a formidable task. It is easy to dream up new things for chips to do, but intensive effort, assisted by computers – themselves made from chips – is needed to work out the details of the design. The manufacturing process needs skill too. Working on the microscopic scale of these devices requires enormous care.

CHECKING THE PATTERN
Although computers carry out much of the design process for chips, the resulting patterns are checked by designers after being printed out by a machine like a gigantic colour photocopier.

MANUFACTURING SEQUENCE
Silicon wafers (p. 36) are turned into integrated circuits by a sequence of operations which includes masking, etching, diffusion, ion implantation (bombarding the wafer with electrically charged atoms), and metallization (to create tracks linking the components). Each wafer may become a hundred or more chips. Just a few of the steps are shown here. Things can go wrong at any stage. A speck of dust can spoil a chip. A processing error can ruin a whole batch of wafers. Getting a good yield of working microchips requires meticulous attention to detail, and can make the difference between the success and failure of a business.

Different colour for each pattern

Transparent plastic sheet

1 SUPERIMPOSED PATTERNS
Extensive checking is essential before embarking on the costly process of chip making. At the early design stages, computers check out the logical design and electrical characteristics of the proposed chip to pinpoint any weaknesses. It is also important that the many superimposed patterns that form the chip line up accurately. For simple chips, transparencies like these can be laid on top of each other to help spot any errors.

Control pattern used for testing

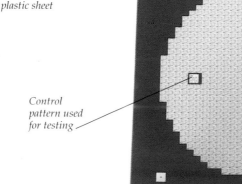

2 PHOTO MASK
A photo mask is used to create a microscopic stencil on the wafer. The wafer is first exposed to oxygen to coat it with impermeable oxide. The photographic process then creates the stencil through which the oxide is etched away. This leaves areas of naked silicon ready to receive the next treatment.

3 DIFFUSING IMPURITIES

Wafers are heated to a high temperature and exposed to chemical compounds which contain the impurity atoms (p. 37) needed to form the parts of the circuit being made at this stage. Batches of wafers are fed into a furnace, where the atoms will diffuse only into those parts of the surface left exposed by the previous masking and etching operations. The wafers will go through many such masking, etching, and diffusion steps before the circuit is complete. Control of time and temperature are critical in diffusion as they have a significant effect on the properties of the finished transistors on the chip. The microscopic scale of these devices requires workers to operate in ultra-clean rooms, masked and gowned like surgeons, because the tiniest speck of dust could prevent a transistor being formed properly.

4 TESTING PROBES

After the entire sequence of steps has been carried out, (including several steps such as metallization which are not shown here), the finished wafers are ready for testing. Every wafer includes a number of control chips which can be tested to ensure that all the steps have been carried out correctly. Individual chips are put through a test cycle. Any that fail are marked for rejection. The tests are carried out by delicate probes operated by a computer. A low failure rate at this stage is crucial if the manufacturing company is to make profits from the chip.

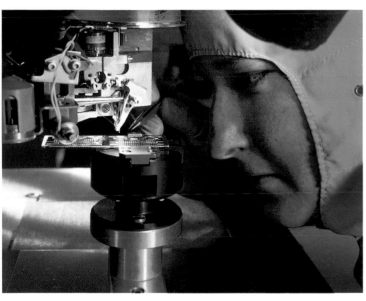

5 BONDING ON WIRES

Individual chips cut from the wafer are now given their links with the outside world. Using a process of cold welding, extremely fine gold wires are bonded on to tiny pads formed around the edges of the chip during the metallization stage. A microscope is needed to line up the chip with the bonding equipment. The automatic process is monitored through the microscope on a television screen. The other ends of the wires will be bonded to the pins that connect the chip to a circuit board.

Plastic packaging

Pin

6 PACKAGING THE CHIP

The chip and its connecting wires are enclosed in a tough plastic or ceramic package. Ceramic packages are used where the chip generates or must withstand high temperatures. This is a small-scale integration chip.

7 PART OF A SYSTEM

The packaged chips are sent out to other manufacturers to build into their products. Integrated circuits of all sizes are needed to make a working system. The large, complex chips do the bulk of the work, but simpler chips, sometimes collectively known as "glue logic", are needed to link these together and control them. The largest chips may each contain over a million transistors.

Connector where board plugs into computer

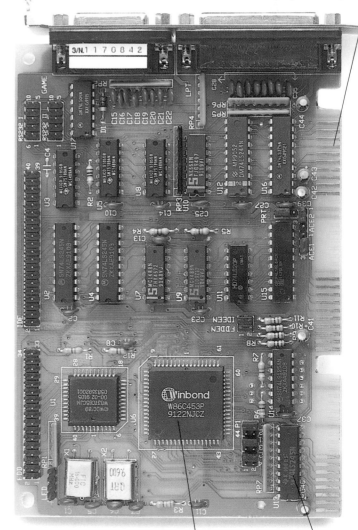

Chips installed in a printed circuit board from a personal computer

Large communications chip

Small "glue logic" chip

How electronic devices remember

THE APPARENT INTELLIGENCE OF COMPUTERS depends largely on a simple ability to remember. Computers do what they are told, but to follow instructions they have to remember them. As they work, they also need to refer to stored information and remember what they have worked out so far. The kind of memory required depends on the kind and quantity of information involved. Programs or data may take up a lot of space and need storing for years. A keyboard remembers most keystrokes for a few thousandths of a second. Data the computer is working on may have to go into or out of memory in 10-millionths of a second. Specialized devices exist for all these purposes.

Records

NON-STOP MUSIC

As well as containing a mass of information stored as music on discs, a juke box has a memory that stores users' requests. Without this, people would have to wait until one record had finished before selecting the next. Memories of this kind are called "buffers". They are needed wherever two devices that work at different speeds have to communicate. Early juke boxes like this one had mechanical memories. Modern machines have fully electronic memories.

FLIP-FLOP SWITCH

A "push-push" switch like the one on this desk lamp is a mechanical flip-flop. It can remember just one bit of information – whether, the last time it was pushed, it turned the light on or off. Whatever it did last time, it does the opposite this time. A set of electronic flip-flops of this kind, with the state of each flip-flop representing one binary digit, can be used for counting.

Codes for selection

Selector buttons

Pressing the switch gives opposite action to the last time

Loudspeaker

Basic memory systems

The simplest electronic memory element, the "flip-flop", was invented as long ago as 1919. It is basically two amplifiers, each with its output connected to the other's input. Thousands of flip-flops together can form a "random-access" memory (RAM). More compact dynamic RAMs (DRAMs) use capacitors (pp. 20-21) to store information. RAMs are needed where data must be stored as well as retrieved, though the data is lost when they are switched off. "Read-only" memories (ROMs), whose contents are fixed during manufacture, are ideal for the programs of microprocessor-controlled machines (pp. 58-59). For sheer storage capacity, much slower magnetic disks beat all these easily.

THE PERSONAL COMPUTER

Memory is fundamental to computing. A personal computer (PC) can be using memory actively even when it seems to be doing nothing. The image on the screen is stored in RAM and is read out many times each second as the cathode ray tube (p. 44) scans. A small program continually cycles through a loop of instructions stored in RAM, waiting for a key to be pressed. A key-press may switch activity to another part of memory, calling up routines that access long-term storage media such as the internal hard disk or removable diskettes holding programs or data.

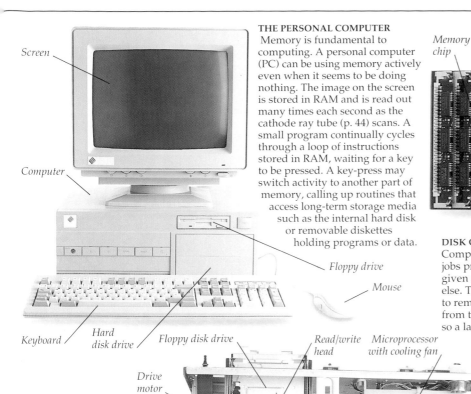

Screen

Computer

Keyboard

Hard disk drive

Floppy disk drive

Floppy drive

Mouse

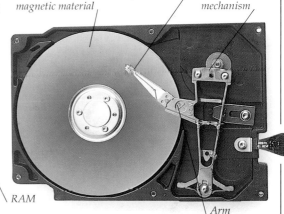

Memory chip

Edge connectors plug into slots in computer

Disk controller

Crystal controls timing

DC-600B   S/N : 1014940

DISK CONTROLLER BOARD

Computers contain specialized circuit boards that deal with jobs presenting a heavy workload. Once the computer has given a task to such a board, it is free to get on with something else. This speeds up the system, but the specialized board has to remember all the details. This board from a PC feeds data from the microprocessor to the disk drives. These work slowly, so a large buffer memory is needed on the board.

INSIDE THE COMPUTER

Looking into this computer, the "floppy" disk drive is easily seen. It works a little like a compact disc player (pp. 46-47), but uses magnetic, not optical, patterns on the surface of removable disks. Hidden underneath is the fixed or hard disk which works in much the same way, but can store a lot more information. The microprocessor (pp. 58-59) also contains substantial amounts of memory. As well as having "registers" that hold the data actually being worked on, it maintains a store of recently used instructions for rapid re-use.

Drive motor

Read/write head

Microprocessor with cooling fan

RAM

Power supply

Slots for extra boards to extend capabilities

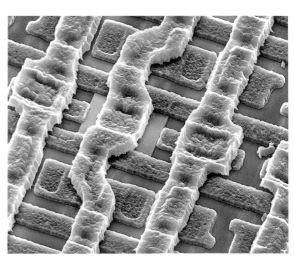

Disk coated with magnetic material

Read/write head

Track selector mechanism

Arm

STORING INFORMATION

Hard disks can store tens of millions of "bytes" (groups of eight binary digits) and retrieve data in a few thousandths of a second. The mechanism is like an agile record player. A magnetic read/write head at the end of the arm is guided by information in a "directory" stored on the disk itself. Data is stored in narrow concentric tracks divided into sectors. The arm moves to a track, then reads the wanted sector of the spinning disk as it passes.

EPROM CHIP

In a complex memory chip, logic (pp. 50-51) selects the "cells" that are to be accessed. Groups of cells each have a number, their "address". The computer sends an address to the chip, which then sends back the data held at that address or stores new data there. This "erasable programmable read-only" memory (EPROM) chip cannot store new data. Until erased by ultraviolet light, it holds information permanently as electric charges.

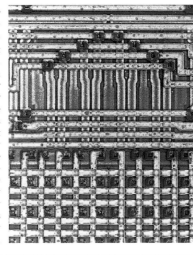

DRAM CHIP

"Dynamic random access" memory (DRAM) chips store information as the presence or absence of charge in microscopic capacitors. This technique gives very small memory cells, allowing millions of binary digits (p. 46) to be stored on one chip. These memories are called "dynamic" because the capacitors are rather leaky, requiring each cell to be read and re-written several hundred times a second. The surface of this chip has been enlarged to 4000 times its actual size.

Microprocessors

As INTEGRATED CIRCUITS BECAME LARGER in the 1970s, they began to present a problem. Bigger circuits are more expensive to design, but are usually more specialized and so have a smaller market. What was needed was one circuit that could do many different things. The answer was the microprocessor – a circuit that could read and act on coded instructions. By storing lists of instructions – programs – in an electronic memory, users could make the same chip do a variety of jobs. The microprocessor is the "brain" of a computer on a single chip. It uses logic (pp. 50-51) to decode instructions and manipulate data as directed. The results can be stored in memory or sent to other devices such as screens or printers. Although revolutionary when it appeared in 1971, the first microprocessor was slow, offered limited memory access and could only handle "words" made up of four binary digits (p. 46). Modern processors can handle 32-bit words, access megabytes of memory, and complete an instruction in a few 10-millionths of a second. Even faster "digital signal processors" are available for specialized tasks, like sending pictures down telephone lines.

COMPUTER ARCHITECTURE

The basic structure of most microprocessors owes much to the work of Hungarian-born American mathematician John von Neumann (1903-1957). Working on early electronic computers in the 1940s, he realized that their instructions and data could both be stored in the same memory, simplifying the structure. Faster but less versatile digital signal processors (DSPs) use separate instruction and data memories to maximize speed.

MICROPROCESSING STAGES

A microprocessor system used to control equipment is basically a small computer, although its program cannot usually be changed by the user. The microprocessor in these scales (below) normally cycles through an instruction loop that continually converts data from the strain gauge and analogue-to-digital (A-to-D) converter (pp. 46-47) to a displayed weight. But it will respond to an "interrupt" caused by the user pressing a button, either to change the units of weight or to store the weight of a container in random-access memory (pp. 56-57) for subtraction from the displayed readings.

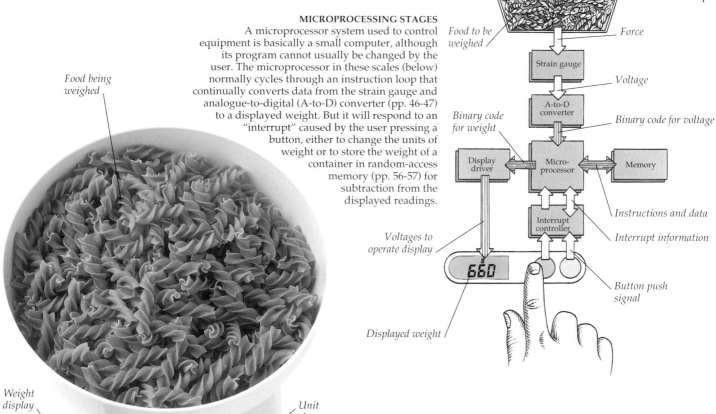

Food being weighed

Food to be weighed

Force

Strain gauge

Voltage

A-to-D converter

Binary code for voltage

Binary code for weight

Display driver

Micro-processor

Memory

Instructions and data

Interrupt controller

Interrupt information

Voltages to operate display

Button push signal

Displayed weight

Weight display

Unit change button

Zero button

SMART SCALES

Microprocessors can make electronic equipment more "intelligent" and easier to use. These scales are a simple example. The processor not only does the arithmetic required to convert the output of a transducer (pp. 42-43) into a weight reading, it can also convert the reading to alternative units or alter its "zero" reading by subtracting the weight of a container. The instructions that control it are held in a read-only memory (pp. 56-57).

DAZZLING MICROCHIP

The apparently blank surface of this microprocessor chip conceals hundreds of thousands of microscopic electronic components with working parts as small as one-thousandth of a millimetre across. These form circuits which include a counter to step through programs, "registers" (single-word memories) to hold data from memory or from calculations, an instruction decoder, an "accumulator" in which arithmetic or logical results are built up, and an "arithmetic logic unit" that does the actual work of combining and transforming data.

ELECTRONIC LEARNING

Very large scale integration (pp. 54-55) has given children computing power once available only to scientists. Built into the read-only memory (ROM) of this microprocessor-controlled educational toy is not only a long list of words to spell, but also several game programs that make learning fun.

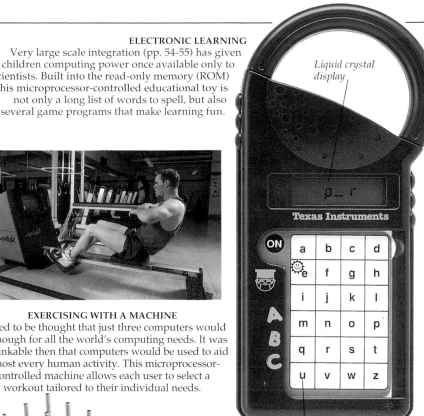

Liquid crystal display

Texas Instruments

Interchangeable cards for different games

EXERCISING WITH A MACHINE

It used to be thought that just three computers would be enough for all the world's computing needs. It was unthinkable then that computers would be used to aid almost every human activity. This microprocessor-controlled machine allows each user to select a workout tailored to their individual needs.

PACKAGED MICROPROCESSOR

Advanced microprocessors need a lot of pins for the "buses" (groups of wires carrying binary words) that connect them to memory and other devices, so even a large microprocessor chip is small compared with the connections and packaging that surround it. This package is 50 mm (2 in) square. The 12 mm (0.5 in) square microprocessor inside repeats a cycle of fetching, decoding, and executing instructions millions of times each second, and can also deal with an "interrupt" (p. 58), then return to what it was doing.

8237635UAB   247   X

Array of pins fits into circuit board

Chip sealed under metal cover

Ceramic package

VISUAL EAR

Microprocessors have turned theory into reality for many professions. Speech therapists can use this equipment to help someone with impaired hearing improve their speech. It creates pictures of the sounds the patient makes, drawing on ideas available for many years but impractical until now.

A SUPERCOMPUTER

This mighty supercomputer does not use microprocessors to perform the massive calculations needed to simulate the behaviour of a nuclear power station – they are much too slow. But there are some microprocessors inside. The computer depends on them to look after the power and cooling systems concealed under the seats that surround it. Without these, the supercomputer would not stay up and running.

A different way of life

People in the industrialized world depend on electronics throughout the day. A quartz clock bleeps a morning alarm, a microwave oven heats a meal, a television set provides evening relaxation. Other electronic systems marshal air and road traffic, get products onto supermarket shelves, and link a billion telephones. Little of modern life is untouched by electronic technology, yet the rate of development can leave people feeling stranded, as the simple and familiar is constantly replaced by the complex and new. This is tolerated because electronics does deliver useful things. Anyone with the right equipment can now take an excellent photograph, quickly call up a friend on the other side of the globe, or even fax them a birthday greeting. Things people buy are better designed and cost less. Their work and their workplace can become lighter and cleaner, while at home news and sport is flashed to them from all over the world.

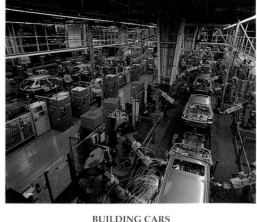

BUILDING CARS
Robots are machines that use electronic memory (pp. 56-57) to imitate the movements of human operators. They have been used in increasing numbers since the 1970s. Motorists have benefited from their introduction by driving better-made, better-value cars. The workers who remain in the factory are better off too, because robots now do the dull and dangerous jobs.

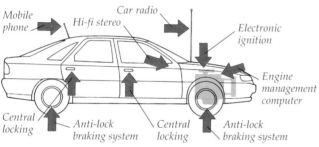

Mobile phone · Car radio · Hi-fi stereo · Electronic ignition · Engine management computer · Central locking · Anti-lock braking system · Central locking · Anti-lock braking system

ELECTRONICS IN THE CAR
The basic design of the car has not changed for 60 years, but its electrical and electronic systems have improved enormously. Car radios were available in the 1930s, but electronic systems that were reliable enough to form part of the car itself were a breakthrough of the 1970s. Digital systems can now monitor and control engine and brakes for greater efficiency and safety, as well as providing convenient security systems and sophisticated communications equipment.

PORTABLE SATELLITE TERMINAL
This journalist's portable satellite terminal connects his computer to a newspaper office thousands of kilometres away. The satellite he is using can be accessed directly, rather than through a ground station (p. 13). The microwave signal (pp. 40-41) is sent out by an antenna under the white dome.

Battery compartment at the back · Television control · Edit and code setting · Liquid crystal display · Timer and clock control · Number keypad · Teletext operation · Video recorder controls · Lid opened to access buttons

VIDEO REMOTE CONTROL
Communicating with electronic equipment can be frustrating. This remote control sends pulses of infra-red light to a video recorder, which can decode them to tell which key was pressed. But its microprocessor (pp. 58-59) offers so many possibilities that the control's small display is hardly adequate to tell the user what is going on. It represents the sort of electronic technology many people dislike. Some of its features will probably never be used.

FACSIMILES

The first fax machine was designed in 1843. Fax was widely used from about 1925 onward for newspaper pictures, and in some businesses from the 1960s. But only in the 1980s, when ingenious coding systems using microprocessors (pp. 58-59) had been developed, could a fast, inexpensive fax machine be built to transmit graphic images down an ordinary telephone line. A feature of fax is its ability to cross international time and language barriers. Images can be sent with a time delay, and the recipient can translate foreign phrases at leisure. Fax is popular in Japan, where the writing system does not lend itself to other forms of transmission.

Telephone handset

Keypad

Liquid crystal display

brother FAX-160

Documents fed in here to be scanned for transmission

Fax received on heat-sensitive paper

American sprinter Carl Lewis winning the 100 m sprint

THE FASTEST TIME

Electronic technology feeds the modern obsession with time. In competitive sport, records are broken and reputations are made with performances measured in milliseconds (p. 23). There is little point in measuring time so accurately if other factors are not taken into account. Electronic equipment will also check the length of the track and monitor the temperature and wind speed. Electronic analyzers check for the presence of drugs in the athletes' blood, and the breaking of a record will be noted in an electronic database.

SPECIAL EFFECTS

The Walt Disney film *Tron* (1982) was the first major production to make extensive use of computer-generated special effects. Earlier animated films were laboriously built up, frame by frame, by armies of artists. They were limited to images that could be created with brush and paint. The computer has opened up a new world of fantasy, not just for film directors, but also for the millions who play video games. But few technologies ever disappear completely. The sound track on this print of *Tron* uses a system invented in the 1920s.

Frame

Sound track

DEFENCE SYSTEMS

Not the ultimate video game, but a real command and communication centre on an aircraft carrier of the US Navy. As well as the conventional orange radar screens (p. 40), it has several computers to keep track of the data coming in. Electronic warfare is a growing area, both warning of threats and, when required, delivering them. But with nothing to see except an electronic display, how real would the resultant destruction seem?

The future of electronics

IN THE PRE-ELECTRIC WORLD, change was rare. Printing, the communications revolution of the 1450s, remained fundamentally unaltered for over 500 years. But electronics began to transform printing in the 1960s, and now, with awesome means of electronic computing and communication at our command, frequent change is the norm in all areas of life. Last year's model is a museum piece. Companies have become international. Instant, inexpensive communication has intensified competition, while desk-top computing has given the power of mathematics to every manager. Electronics itself is not immune to accelerated change. Valves (p. 28) dominated electronic technology for 50 years. Transistors, as separate components, gave way to integrated circuits (pp. 52-53) after 25 years. Now, electronics is giving birth to a new technology – photonics. Springing from the technology of fibre-optic communications, photonics promises to control light with light, giving the possibility of future all-optical computers many times faster than their electronic ancestors.

Type locked up to form a page

Block for printing picture

Print made from an inked block

LASER PRINTER
Today, ideas can get from author to reader by a route bypassing traditional printing operations. Keystrokes memorized on a computer disk (p. 57) access another memory that holds the shapes of letters and pictures, driving a laser printer that can put fully fledged documents straight on to paper. A fax machine (p. 63) or direct fax link can create a copy any distance away in seconds.

LETTERPRESS PRINTING
In spite of mechanization, printing did not change fundamentally for over 500 years after its invention around 1450. Lines of metal type were assembled into pages, following the author's manuscript, then inked and pressed on to paper in a press. Image reproduction changed more. Blocks were originally engraved by hand, but by 1900 photographic engraving was common.

Controls

Liquid crystal display

Laser-printed document

Paper feed

Printer has its own memory storing letter shapes

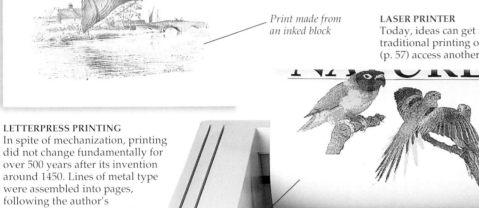

A4

FIBRE-OPTIC CABLE

Fibre optics began to be important in the late 1970s as the limited capacity of copper cables threatened to throttle the expanding communications network. After attempts to use waveguides (p.41) to link city centres, it was realized that laser light, pulse-code modulated (p. 46) and travelling in hair-fine glass fibres, could offer almost unlimited communication capacity. Fibre-optic links have now replaced cables on most major telephone and data routes.

Insulating plastic covering

Optical fibre

"UNPLANNED OBSOLESCENCE"

Electronic technology ages rapidly. This valve computer, used for business management rather than scientific calculation, was considered advanced in 1953, but its computing power was comparable to that of a modern programmable hand-held calculator.

INSTALLING FIBRE-OPTIC CABLE

New technologies demand new skills, and workers must adapt or move on. It has taken several years for reliable ways of joining and handling fine glass fibres to be developed. Though the fibres are tough, any kinks allow light to leak out, causing the signal to lose power. To avoid this, fibres can be wafted into ducts, as here, by a stream of air.

Earpiece

Liquid crystal display

Keypad

Microphone

MOBILE PHONE

The telephone was tied down by wires when it appeared in 1876. Now computers have let it off the leash. Mobile phones are possible because a network of radio transmitters can, under computer control, use the same scarce frequencies many times over. Inexpensive phones like this one can only make one-way calls, but by the year 2000 advanced pocket communicators will probably be commonplace.

COMPUTER-AIDED DESIGN

It used to be difficult to communicate the shapes designers wanted to the people who make the tools that press car bodies out of metal. Now that computers can calculate and specify every point of a three-dimensional curve – here a computer printout is being scrutinized – fashion in car design is changing from a rather boxy look to something much smoother.

OVERSEEING EARTH

Electronics has given us a new world view. Without computers and communications there would be no space satellites. Without satellite pictures, often delivered by electronic technology, most people would not think of their planet as the small and vulnerable place it is. The invention of printing ushered in a long period in which people thought they could use knowledge to shape the world. Electronics has shown them otherwise.

Index

Acknowledgments

Dorling Kindersley would like to thank:
John Becklake, Stewart Emmens, Stephen Foulger, Ian Carter and Science Museum Library Staff, Brian Gilliam and object handling team, Derek Hudson, Douglas Millard, Peter Stephens, and Anthony Wilson for advice and help with the provision of objects for photography at the Science Museum; Karl Adamson, Dave King, Philip Gatward, and Visual 7 for photography; Printing paraphernalia (p. 62) lent by the John Jarrold Printing Museum, Norwich; Sony and Walkman (p. 53b) are registered trademarks of Sony Corporation, Japan; spectrum analyzer photographs throughout the book by courtesy of Marconi Instruments Ltd; juke box on p. 56r from RS Leisure Ltd, The Jukebox

Showroom, London NW10; printed circuit boards (pp 17 & 23) from Somerville CDO Circuits, London SE16; Gregory Jennings, Imperial College for help with the oscilloscope images; Dixons, London for the loan of electronic equipment on pp. 3r, 4bl, 7t, 41t, 63r; Dr. Bryson Gore and Bipin Parmar at The Royal Institution for allowing us to photograph the wave machine on pp. 14-15; Peter Ramiz and the staff at MESH for computing equipment on pages 45b, 53br, 55br, 57c, 62b; GEC Plessey Semiconductors for objects on p 54b; Olympus for the camera on p. 21b; GEC-Marconi Research Centre for the SAW filter on p. 35t.

Illustrations John Woodcock; Nick Hall; Stephen Bull; Roy Flooks
Index Jane Parker

Picture credits
t=top b=bottom c=centre l=left r=right

Allsport 8c; 48tr; 59tc; 61cl. Aquarius Picture Library 46cr. Arcaid 51tr. Associated University Presses/*PaulEisler: My Life with the printed circuit* 23cr. Courtesy of A.T.&T. Archives 31tr; 38br; 49tr. Copyright © BBC 27tr. Bettmann Archive/UPI 40tl; 48br; /UPI 58tr. BT Museum 25tc. BT pictures; a BT photograph 47c; 63tr. Capel Manor 33tl. Colorsport 44tl. Jean Loup Charmet 12tl; 14cl. Mary Evans Picture Library 8tl; 9tr; 20tl; 22cl; 24br; 26c; 42tl; 46tl; 50tl. Ronald Grant Archive 6tr; 9tr; 61tcr. Robert Harding Picture Library 41tr; 43br; 45cl; 60tr. Hulton Deutsche 11tc; 28bl; 36tr; 37tl; 42bc; 63tl. Image Bank 17bl. Imperial War Museum 40bl. Jane's Information Group 61bl. Magnum Photos/Erwitt 20cl. Mansell Collection 19cl; 26tl. Northern Telecom Europe Limited/STC Archives 47cl. Popperphoto 30tr; 30cr; 38tl. Science Museum Library 13c; 29cl. Science Photo Library/Simon Fraser 7tcr;

7cr; 9bcr; 10tr; 13cr; 16tl; 25tl; /P.Parviainen 26br; /Occidental Consortium 28br; /William Curisger 33br; 36c; /Simon Fraser 36bc; 45cr; /Dr Jeremy Burgess 47tl; /Andrew Syred 47tr; Alfred Pasleka 51br; /Manfred Cage 53c; /Takeshi Takahara 54tl; /David Parker 55tl; /David Parker 55cl; /Ray Ellis 55tr; /Jeremy Burgess 56bl; /David Scharfe 57br; /James King Holmes 59bl; /David Parker 59br; /George Haling 63cl; /NASA 63bc.Texas Instruments Ltd 53tc. Zefa 35tl; 59tl; 60l.

With the exception of the items listed above, and the objects on pages 1, 6b, 7b, 11b, 12c, 15b, 16l, 17b, 19r, 19c, 21t, 23t, 31r, 34t, 36l, 37r, 38cr, 39c, 40cl, 43b, 46b, 47b, 49b, 50/51c, 56l, 58l, 59t 60b, 61t, all the photographs in this book are of objects in the collections of the Science Museum, London.